MAKING STORIES

A Practical Guide
for Organizational Leaders and
Human Resource Specialists

Terrence L. Gargiulo

QUORUM BOOKS
Westport, Connecticut · London

Library of Congress Cataloging-in-Publication Data

Gargiulo, Terrence L., 1968–
   Making stories : a practical guide for organizational leaders and human resource
specialists / Terrence L. Gargiulo.
      p.   cm.
   Includes bibliographical references and index.
   ISBN 1–56720–381–7 (alk. paper)
   1. Personnel management.   2. Fiction—Social aspects.   3. Fiction—Psychological aspects.
I. Title.
HF5549.G3174   2002
658.3—dc21   2001019591

British Library Cataloguing in Publication Data is available.

Library of Congress Catalog Card Number: 2001019591
ISBN: 1–56720–381–7

First published in 2002

Quorum Books, 88 Post Road West, Westport, CT 06881
An imprint of Greenwood Publishing Group, Inc.
www.quorumbooks.com

Printed in the United States of America

The paper used in this book complies with the
Permanent Paper Standard issued by the National
Information Standards Organization (Z39.48–1984).

10   9   8   7   6   5   4   3   2   1

To "mio padre e mio maestro"
for instilling in me a passion for communication
and to Luis Yglesias
for opening my eyes to the magic of stories.

Contents

Preface ix

PART I Entering the Story Paradigm

1 Introduction 3

2 Stories Empower Speakers, Create an
Environment, and Help People Bond 11

3 Stories Engage Our Minds in Active Listening
and Allow Us to Negotiate Differences 19

4 Stories Encode Information, Are Tools for
Thinking, Serve as Weapons, Bring about Healing 31

**PART II Putting Stories to Work in Human Resources,
Training, and Organizational Development**

5 The Role Stories Can Play in Human Resources 41

6 Using Stories in Training 53

7 Exercises to Develop Story Skills That Can
Be Used in Training 61

8 The Role of Stories in Business Processes
and Knowledge Management 79

9 The Role of Stories in Corporate Culture,
Change Management, and Leadership 87

PART III A Practical Guide to Developing the "Story Mind"

10 The "Story Mind"   99

11 Building an Index of Personal Stories   105

12 Exercises in Business Observations:
An Example of the Relationship between
Stories and Behavior   135

APPENDIXES

A Additional Vignettes to Illustrate the
Story Paradigm   151

B Summary of the Story Model   163

C The Story of Lilly   165

D Ordering Story Cards and
Obtaining More Information   173

Suggested Reading   175

Index   177

Preface

Stories are all around us. I am going to ask you to take a marvelous journey with me, but before we start, you must leave behind any preconceived ideas you may have about what a story is.

I'll never forget one of my first classes at Brandeis University. One of the requirements was a two-semester humanities class. I must confess I was less than excited about the class. It looked as though it was going to be a waste of time. Nothing could have been further from the truth.

I ended up in a class being taught by Professor Luis Yglesias titled "Imagining Who We Are." Professor Yglesias began his class by reading Shel Silverstein's story, *The Giving Tree*. It's a simple story about a boy and a tree growing up together. The tree is always there for the boy. In the end the tree even gives its life so that the boy can build a home for himself with its wood.

As he finished, the entire class sighed sentimentally. But Professor Yglesias did not stop. He returned to the first page of the story and reread it to us. Without editorializing, using only his mischievous eyes and the nuances of his voice, he brought the story alive in a completely different way.

Imagine our surprise when we realized that *The Giving Tree* was not necessarily a sweet story. The boy could as easily be seen as narcissistic and exploitive; the tree knew how to give, but the boy only took.

The same story that had greatly moved the class was now responsible for catalyzing emotions of outrage and disbelief. Some of us were angry for having our idealized vision of the boy and the tree shattered; some of us were incensed by the social message of selfishness and the abuse of nature implied by the story.

Professor Yglesias was not making a political comment. Nor was he trying to espouse postmodern assertions of relativism. He was simply giving us a wake-up call, and he was activating our imaginations. He was guiding us to actively connect to the story, and he was asking us to challenge our habitual response to the sort of story we had heard many times. We were being led to discover the heart of what stories are all about. My life has not been the same since that day.

You see, stories do not fit into neat cubbyholes of meaning. Stories are a tool for reflection and insight. Stories graciously offer us the opportunity to look at ourselves and the world around us in new ways.

My first objective in this book is to persuade you to suspend any preconceived ideas you have about what a story is. I will apologize now to anyone who is looking for me to define stories in a scientific way. I will point out all of the things stories are, but I will not offer you a "be all–end all" definition; that would betray the very essence of stories.

ACKNOWLEDGMENTS

Behind every effort there are countless stories. I am indebted to so many people for their time, ideas, and encouragement. My mother has been tireless and selfless with her love and her belief in me. My beloved wife Cindy inspired me every step of the way. My sister Franca was always willing to give me a reality check. Maria Sachs and Bill Gleason kept my writing on track. My editor Eric Valentine helped me focus my ideas and express them with clarity. Discussions with Bill Zornes challenged me to look at things from multiple perspectives. And last but not least, a big thank you to everyone who has touched my life: you've all given me stories.

PART I

Entering the
Story Paradigm

Chapter 1

Introduction

Stories are fundamental to the way we *learn* and to the way we *communicate*. They are the most efficient way of storing, retrieving, and conveying information. Since story hearing requires active participation by the listener, stories are the most profoundly social form of human interaction and communication.

Today, more than ever, market pressures force organizations to constantly change and adapt. It is tempting to believe that the tools of technology can meet today's market challenges head on. But unless an organization can communicate and learn, there is very little that technology can do. Leaders need processes and strategies to get an accurate read on their company and to communicate new visions and missions to employees.

Stories can be used strategically to galvanize an organization in a lot of different ways. Advertisers have always understood the power of stories. Take the following example:

> A new company wants to enter the butter market. It wants to sell richly flavored butters. What story can the company tell to position its product and capture the attention of consumers?
>
> Well, to begin with, let's imagine packaging the butter in old-fashioned miniature crocks. Next, let's use a "grandfather" figure to be our spokesman. We'll have grandfather spreading butter on a warm piece of toast while he remi-

nisces about his childhood memories of fresh, rich butter in crocks being brought by Farmer Brown who would come into town with his horse and buggy delivering butter from house to house.

In this simple example we have a perfect illustration of how stories index information and elicit images in the minds of others. Here's a quick breakdown of what's going on in the story.

Image	Function
Grandfather	Wise elderly figure, full of memories, counteracting any conception of butter being bad for one's health.
Grandfather's memories	Elicits yearning for the good old days, farms, freshness, wholesomeness, and grandfather.
Crocks	Magic objects that "satisfy" nostalgic yearning.

And it's not only in advertising that stories work well. The following list gives a quick bird's-eye view of some of the other ways:

When are stories applicable in business?	How are stories used in business?	Who uses stories in business?
Presenting	Animating talks and presentations	Leaders
	Anchoring a message	Public relations
	Potentiating a message	Sales
		Marketing
Imaging	Product positioning	Marketing
	Appealing to an audience	Advertising
	Dialoguing with customers	Sales
	Innovating	Customer service
		Research and development
Connecting	Pacing—getting in sync with others	Sales
	Recruiting	Market research
	Discovering talents of employees	Human resources
	Problem solving	Managers, leaders
	Finding the critical point in a system	

Learning	Training	Trainers
	Developing staff	Human resources
	Knowledge management	Organizational developers
	Change management	Managers, leaders
Leading–staff development	Building and managing corporate culture	Trainers
	Mentoring and coaching	Human resources
	Engendering loyalty	Managers, leaders
	Cultivating diversity	
Team building	Energizing employees	Team leaders
	Creating synergy	Managers
	Collaborating	
	Partnering	

One book cannot possibly cover all of the business areas in which stories can be used. This book focuses on showing human resources professionals and executives some of the ways they can put the power of stories to work for them.

TOWARD A "NONDEFINITION OF STORIES"

For those of you who would like a more systematic framework for beginning your study of stories, let me offer some insights from Roger Schank, director of the Institute of Learning at Northwestern University:

> Stories are everywhere, but not all stories look like stories. If you consider a story to be a previously prepared gist of something to say, something that you have said before or heard another say, then a great deal of conversation is simply mutual storytelling. Moreover, if the majority of what we say is in our memories in the form of previously prepared stories, the way we look at the nature of understanding and what it means to be intelligent must change. Is being very intelligent just having a great many stories to tell? Is it adapting superficially irrelevant stories into relevant ones, i.e., finding a story in one domain and applying it by analogy to another? Maybe it means combining stories and making generalizations from them—or, perhaps intelligence is embodied in the initial process of collecting

stories to tell in the first place. (Roger Schank, *Tell Me A Story: A New Look at Real and Artificial Memory* [Evanston, Ill.: Northwestern University Press, 1995], 26–27)

There is a lot to digest in this description of stories. Schank began his research in artificial intelligence, and in order to create a thinking machine, he set out to understand how the mind works. He concluded that our minds work in stories. He asserts that stories are all around us. Any time we open our mouths and respond to another person in a conversation, we are accessing memories. These memories are not stored as discrete facts; they are stored as stories.

We could not possibly hold in our minds all of the data that a computer stores. Think about the disk drive of your computer. All of your documents have been reduced to zeros and ones. Every zero and one must be stored. A computer needs all of the details to restore your word processing document or spreadsheet to the computer's active memory.

Does your mind work in the same way? Absolutely not. Our minds are immeasurably more complex. They do not store all the details the way a computer does. When you recall an experience, your mind takes a chunk of information and reconstructs all of the details for you. Therefore our mind is incredibly efficient. Furthermore, our mind is capable of synthesizing information in new ways. We apply our knowledge or experience from one area to another area.

Schank suggests that intelligence is not defined by the collection or storage of a lot of information but rather by our ability to index our experiences in multiple ways and our capacity for discovering the relationships between experiences in different domains. The hallmark of intelligence is our ability to collect stories and regularly reflect on them in order to continually gain new insights from them.

One of the common misconceptions about stories is that they are used only to convey an intended message. Certainly, stories can be used to communicate a predigested message such as a moral; but to limit stories to such simplistic forms of communication is to miss out on a whole array of nuances and possibilities. Stories interplay with one another. The same story can evoke totally different responses in different people.

Stories do not always begin with the words "once upon a time." Stories can be as short as one or two sentences. They may not even be expressed in words. In fact, a basic premise of stories is that through them we "enact" rather than "announce" our intentions, thoughts, values, or knowledge. Essentially, stories allow us to model what we want to communicate instead of having to explain it.

Let's agree to broaden our notion of what a story is, and throughout the book let's examine stories across the following five dimensions:

- Communication
- Learning
- Memory
- Imagination
- Intelligence

THE STRUCTURE AND ORGANIZATION OF THE BOOK

Story thinking requires us to use muscles that over the course of time have atrophied terribly in most of us. All of us would have been using stories more effectively in organizations if it were simply a matter of intellectually understanding a concept, or if someone had laid out all of the steps; but it's not that easy.

This book is divided into three parts. In the first part, I describe how stories work. This is the most important part. There will be a temptation to skim this section and skip to other sections of the book that are more detailed and practical in nature. Don't do that.

Part I presents a model of how stories are used and their effects. Each chapter offers vignettes or examples. On the surface, the individual vignettes are deceptively easy. Taken as a whole they will experientially move you towards a new paradigm. We will use the vignettes to synthesize a model of how and why stories work. Our task is to understand how these uses and effects are interconnected and interact with one another. Here is a breakdown of the story uses:

1. Stories empower a speaker.
2. Stories create an environment.
3. Stories bind and bond individuals.
4. Stories engage our minds in active listening.
5. Stories negotiate differences.
6. Stories encode information.
7. Stories are tools for thinking.
8. Stories serve as weapons.
9. Stories bring about healing.

Some of these uses are illustrated with vignettes. A short analysis follows each. Additional vignettes are offered in Appendix A. As you read the vignettes, think about your own experiences.

Throughout the book we will refer to the story model to understand how to practically apply the power of stories to business interactions. The "story paradigm" model is the foundation of this book. Experientially understanding and engaging that model will unleash a wealth of insights and possibilities.

Part II suggests how human resource managers can use stories to understand business processes, how to develop competency models, and how to incorporate stories into training. Chapter 5 explores the various ways stories apply to human resources. Chapters 6 and 7 offer training managers and curriculum developers specific story exercises and techniques to use in training. Chapter 8 looks at how to use stories to capture, analyze, and understand business processes. Chapter 9 deals with the role stories play in effective leadership. We will look at how to use stories to create and manage corporate culture, effect change management, and develop future leaders. You will learn how to scan stories you collect for incongruence between the stated or desired corporate culture, the actual corporate culture, and either the positive or negative impact of your company's policies on corporate culture. We will see how stories are an effective communication tool for managing change in an organization as well as for guiding and supporting employees as they struggle with uncertainty, ambiguity, and chaos. The last part of Chapter 9 highlights the important role stories play in helping leaders build rapport, teach, and maintain excellent relationships with the employees they coach and mentor.

Part III explores the various levels on which stories work. In this section we move from the theoretical to the practical. Chapter 10 puts everything together and presents a model of the "story mind." Chapter 11 offers a series of exercises to build a large index of personal stories, and Chapter 12 examines the relationship between stories and behavior.

GETTING TO THE TRUTH OF THE STORY

Allow me to set the stage for our journey. It's only appropriate that we should end this introduction with a story.

> Thomas had done it all. At the age of fifty he had become CEO of a Fortune 100 company; he had a beautiful family, and all of the material things he could ever want. However, there was a gnawing question in Thomas's mind. He remembered as a young boy listening to a gospel story about Jesus. In the story, Jesus is asked, "What is Truth?" Tho-

mas had always wondered why Jesus never replied. So one day, Thomas turned to his wife and said, "Honey, I am so happy. Our life is wonderful. But I need to go on a quest for Truth."

"Well, honey," she replied, "if it is important to you I think you should go. I'll pack you a nice lunch, and you can give me power of attorney, and then you can head out tomorrow morning."

The next morning, Thomas took his lunch and hit the road. He left his BMW in the garage; somehow he thought he should conduct his pilgrimage on foot. So Thomas walked and walked. He stopped at his company's manufacturing plant. He had heard that workers hold the keys to Truth but he found no Truth there. Next he went to the White House. He found a lot of hot air but no Truth. Then he stopped at the Vatican to speak with the Pope, but again he found no Truth. On and on he wandered, until he found himself in a very remote part of the world. At long last he saw a sign with an arrow pointing up a hill. The sign read, "Truth This Way."

Thomas stumbled up the hill and came to a little shack with a blinking marquee, "The Truth Lives Here." He nervously knocked on the door.

A moment later the door began to creak open. Thomas craned his neck around the corner to get his first glimpse of Truth. What he saw made him jump back five feet. Standing before him was the oldest, most hideous creature he had ever seen. It was all hunched over. In a high-pitched, cackling voice, it said, "Yes, dear?"

"Oh, I am terribly sorry, I think I have the wrong house. I was looking for Truth."

The creature smiled and said, "Well, you've found me. Please come inside."

So Thomas went inside and began to learn about Truth. For years Thomas stayed by the creature's side, absorbing all of the intricacies of Truth. He was amazed at the things he learned. Then one day he turned to it and said, "Truth, I have learned so much from you, but now I must go home and share my wisdom and knowledge with others. I do not know where to begin. What should I tell people?"

The hideous old creature leaned forward and said, "Well, dear, tell them I am young and beautiful."

In the words of Mark Twain, "Sometimes you have to lie a little bit to tell the truth."

Chapter 2

Stories Empower Speakers, Create an Environment, and Help People Bond

STORIES EMPOWER A SPEAKER

Jack approached the podium with confidence. He could not believe it had been over twenty years since his high school graduation. The perfunctory applause died down, and Jack's eyes met the stares of over five hundred students awaiting his words of wisdom.

Jack took a beat of silence and then raised his fist in the air and yelled, "Shazam!" into the microphone. Without waiting for his startled audience to settle back in their seats, Jack continued.

"Ms. Coldenfish was her name. Paints, charcoal, and papier maché were the game. Room 62, second period, on Mondays and Thursdays, this was my junior year nightmare. I must have flunked preschool, because to this day I cannot draw a circle and color it yellow inside. To avoid sinking into a pool of artistic self-contempt I used art class as an opportunity to religiously pursue one of my favorite subjects: flirting! Ms. Coldenfish and I had very different agendas. She could not understand how anyone could resist being drawn into her world of shapes, colors, and perspectives. I could not understand why she insisted on trying to sell us on her passion, even as she persisted in interfering with mine.

"Art was her strength, and discipline was her weakness. Whenever our class got out of control, Ms. Coldenfish would yell 'Shazam!' Perhaps some of you have seen a TV show called *The Greatest American Hero*. The main character was your typical nerd by day, superhero by night. Whenever he had to transform himself from nerd to superhero, he would yell his magic word. And what word do you think he yelled?"

Analysis

Every speaker faces the challenge of engaging his audience. Try to recall the most memorable speakers you have heard. Undoubtedly, you are recalling a story or anecdote the speaker used to anchor the talk. Jack remembers what it was like to be a high school student. Jack's story is funny. We are drawn into the picture he paints of art class with his idiosyncratic art teacher. However, there is more than humor in this story. If Jack is merely an accomplished public speaker with all of the skills and techniques of the trade, he may not realize how he can use his story as a leverage to reach deep into the minds of his audience and not just entertain them.

Jack's story allows him to be vulnerable in front of his audience. His talk is to a group of high school students about to take a ceremonial step toward adulthood. Memories of failing art and goofing off in a class taught by a quirky but passionate teacher, reviewed later in life, can yield rich lessons. Jack can now weave a collage of stories and anecdotes that chronicle his maturation. Stories and experiences must be seen in relation to one another. Stories in isolation are deprived of their fullest potential.

STORIES CREATE AN ENVIRONMENT OF TRUST

Phil Anderman, president and CEO of Precision Dynamics, had no idea why his company had fallen on such bad times. Profits were down, morale was low, and interdepartmental feuds threatened to turn a bad situation into a deadly one.

Phil knew he needed to change the organization's culture. Currently, departments were competing for vital resources. The company's structure, which he had put in place, did not encourage the integration of resources. At the time, the strategy had sounded brilliant: encourage innovation and teamwork by fostering a competitive environment. Now, with the luxury of hindsight, he knew he had been wrong.

Tomorrow morning he was to meet with all the departmental heads, and he wasn't sure what he was going to say. Well, first things first, he thought. It was time to tuck his daughter into bed. Morning would come soon enough.

When Phil walked into the conference room the next day, it was buzzing with uncertainty and suspicion. There had been a lot of rumors and people were on edge; so was Phil, for that matter.

"Good morning everyone. Please take a seat so we can get started; we have a lot to discuss. Last night I sat at home agonizing about what I should say this morning. As I was tucking my seven-year-old daughter Maya into bed, she shared with me a story she had heard at school. It goes something like this.

"There once was a farmer. After working all morning in the scorching sun, he sat down under a shady tree to take a rest. Wiping the sweat from his eyes, the farmer thought, 'Oh, I wish I had some cool, clear water to splash on my face.' Suddenly a pail of water fell from the tree, drenching the farmer below.

"'That felt so good,' the farmer said to himself. 'I just wish I had some more water to quench my thirst.' This time a bucket of water appeared by his side. Now, the farmer was no dummy. He knew that he had stumbled upon a wishing tree and that he had only one wish left. Lifting his voice to the leaves above, he said, 'I want to meet the wisest teacher.'

"Before he had even completed uttering his wish, a robed figure appeared before him. He asked the farmer, 'What would you like to learn or see?'

"Without hesitation, the farmer replied, 'I want to learn how to get to heaven.'

"The teacher's sparkling blue eyes flashed, and suddenly the ground in front of the farmer opened up with a fierce rumble and an escalator leading downward appeared. The farmer asked the wise teacher, 'Where will this take us?'

"The teacher smiled and said, 'The way to heaven is through hell.'

"They both stepped onto the escalator and began their descent. At last they saw a sign that read, 'Welcome to Hell—Banquet Hall Straight Ahead.' The farmer was awfully hungry from the long trip. He turned to the teacher and said, 'Let's go get some food.'

"They headed for the banquet hall. As they entered, the farmer stopped in his tracks at the magnificent sight. There were long marble tables with large vases filled with bright and sweet-smelling flowers. Each table held dozens of gold trays heaped with the most delectable foods.

"The farmer turned to the teacher and said, 'I don't understand.'

"'Look very carefully,' responded the teacher.

"The farmer suddenly noticed food flying all over the place. People were swarming from one table to another grabbing food from golden trays. Then the farmer saw what the teacher wanted him to observe; the elbows of each person were permanently locked straight. People were attempting to eat the food from the trays by throwing it in the air and then trying to catch it in their mouths. As a result, food was flying everywhere and very little of it was actually getting eaten.

"In a pleading voice the farmer said, 'May we go now? I have seen enough.'

"The teacher nodded, and in the wink of an eye they were on another escalator and climbing into the sky. At long last it stopped by a sign that read, 'Welcome to Heaven—Banquet Hall Straight Ahead.'

"So the teacher and farmer went to the banquet hall, and again the farmer stopped dead in his tracks. The banquet hall was identical to the one in hell, with long, marble tables decorated with large vases filled with bright and sweet-smelling flowers and gold trays heaped with the most delectable foods.

"The teacher guided the farmer toward one of the tables. As the farmer approached he felt his elbows lock straight. Glancing around the room, he realized that everyone was in the same predicament. Even the teacher's arms could not bend. The teacher spoke: 'We are hungry. Let us eat.' With that, he picked up a piece of food and extended it toward the farmer's mouth. The farmer did likewise, and they ate to their hearts' content. When the farmer had chewed his last morsel of food, he found himself, once again, in the shade of the wishing tree.

"'I'm afraid I have neither a wishing tree nor wisdom to offer you. We are going through some tough times. I realize that we have not always made the best decisions, or implemented the best policies, but I firmly believe we can get through this. Before we dive into the strategic plan, would someone please pass me the coffee?'"

Analysis

Phil recognizes the relevance of the story his daughter heard in school to his company's predicament. He shows us how a story or experience becomes an opportunity for reflection and insight. Phil's receptivity to the story is a defining characteristic of the "story mind"; it does not matter that the story comes from a child. The story mind develops the discipline of synthesizing information. While on the surface there may be no apparent connection, the story mind looks for relationships between ideas and concepts from different areas and experiences.

Phil decides that he does not need to put up a false front of strength and leadership in order to motivate his managers. On the surface, he risks appearing vulnerable by alluding to the ineffective policies he instated that encouraged competition between departments, by expressing his uncertainty and apprehensions about the company's present position, and by sharing a story told to him by his daughter. But that very vulnerability and use of the story creates an environment of trust. The story encapsulates the changes the company will need to embrace in order to regain market share. And deliberately or not, Phil ends his story by asking someone to pass him the coffee. To Phil, the "The way to heaven is through hell" story is not just an allegorical tale; it is a template for his thinking and communication.

What if Phil had said this instead: "We all know that Precision Dynamics has fallen on hard times. Sometimes a company needs to go through a little hell before it can reap the benefits of growth. Now more than ever you need to pull together as a team and do whatever it takes to beat the market's down cycle. We will not allow our competitors to push their way into our value chains. Today I will take you through our strategic plan for the next quarter. It is imperative that you follow the road map set out in this plan. Precision Dynamics's success rests in your hands."

Here Phil sounds like a no-nonsense CEO. He gets to his point quickly and tells his managers what they need to do. But is he as effective? The tone is dictatorial. When was the last time you changed your behavior because of a motivating speech someone made? Words can be silvery; all of us can be moved by a person's charisma and rhetoric, but we rarely identify with the speaker or undergo a significant shift within ourselves. Phil's tone and words are unlikely to elicit the response he seeks. He is presenting a strategy of teamwork, but he is clearly setting himself apart from the team.

A colleague of mine was once named director of a dysfunctional department. For years people had been bickering and fighting. Over the course of a year and a half, things improved. At the department's annual holiday party, my colleague decided to tell the "The way to heaven is through hell" story and act it out with his staff assistant.

The response was unbelievable. Managers came up to them after the party and said, "Thank you for showing us the way out of hell."

STORIES BIND AND BOND INDIVIDUALS

Michael Moore ended his telephone conversation and headed toward the elevators. As CEO and chairman, he had called a press conference for Wall Street financial analysts to go over the company's third-quarter revenue projections. Prospects looked good, and he wanted to get the word out on the street.

Jerry Johnson fumbled his way out of the human resources department and stopped for a moment to check his clipboard. His next stop was the executive suite on the twenty-eighth floor. He took out his identification badge and pinned it to his shirt; he would need it to gain access to the offices on that floor.

This was Jerry's second week at Allbright Conglomerate, and he hadn't yet gotten into the swing of things. If delivering mail was this hard, how would he ever climb the corporate ladder and become an executive? he wondered to himself. Jerry stepped into the elevator and absentmindedly thumbed through the packages and envelopes in his cart. He became so engrossed that he didn't notice that the elevator doors had opened on the twenty-eighth floor.

Michael got into the elevator and pressed the button for the lobby. Before Jerry realized what had happened, the doors had closed. "Shoot!" Jerry exclaimed. "I needed to get off on the twenty-eighth floor."

In his frustration, Jerry dropped the mail he was carrying. Jerry shook his head in disgust. Michael, without a second thought, bent down to pick up the dropped mail and handed it to Jerry. He paused for a moment to look into Jerry's eyes.

"Thanks," Jerry muttered self-consciously. He could feel Michael's concerned gaze searching through him. "This is my second week working here, and I'm still trying to learn my delivery route. I am a first-year business studies major at Walton University, but if I keep this up I won't be fit for a job flipping hamburgers."

"I'll never forget my first job," said Michael. "I worked as a receptionist for an automotive company. Have you ever seen one of those old switchboards with plugs and holes?"

"Yeah, you mean like the one featured in that AT&T commercial where the operator is trying to answer a bunch of lines at the same time?" answered Jerry.

"Yes, that was me," Michael mused. "I was the biggest disaster. I could never keep the outgoing lines separated from the incoming lines, and I was constantly hanging up on people. That was the most difficult and chaotic job I have ever had. Certainly taught me to appreciate operators."

The doors of the elevator opened onto the lobby and Michael stepped out. "Good luck, Jerry Johnson," Michael said. "My name is Michael Moore. Let me know how you get on."

Analysis

Stories act as glue between people. In other words, stories show how our sets of experiences, memories, hopes, fears, and desires match with someone else's. I will be able to understand you, and communicate effectively with you, only when I can relate my stories to your stories.

Stories have the power to bind and bond individuals regardless of their relative position or experience. Michael Moore is a busy CEO with an important press conference to get to, and Jerry Johnson is a young kid in his first job as a mail clerk for a big corporation.

Jerry is so preoccupied with trying to figure out how to do his job that he does not realize the elevator has reached the twenty-eighth floor. Frazzled, Jerry drops a bundle of mail. Michael picks it up and looks into Jerry's eyes. He initially tries to connect with Jerry by making eye contact. Naturally Jerry becomes self-conscious and tries to explain his clumsiness.

His explanation triggers a memory, and Michael decides to share a story about his first job. Notice that Michael begins his story in the form of a question. By doing that he is involving Jerry. When Jerry answers, he must transcend his own predicament and vicariously imagine Michael's first job experience as a switchboard operator.

Why doesn't Michael just give Jerry a pep talk? He could have easily said something like, "Well, son, I remember my first job and it wasn't easy. You need to keep your nose to the grindstone and believe in yourself. With hard work and a little luck, who knows? Maybe you'll be CEO of a company one day."

Michael does not give a pep talk because he knows how ineffective it would be. A pep talk would not be the best response. He does not want to distance himself from Jerry; he wants to connect with him. Michael completes the bond by noticing Jerry's name badge. He wishes Jerry good luck and invites him to seek another opportunity to continue their discussion. (Note: Take a look at the vignettes in Appendix A for more examples of how stories bind and bond individuals.)

Footnote

Time and again I have witnessed the magic of people forming bonds with one another during training workshops. I remember one striking example. I was facilitating a workshop for a company that was going through massive layoffs. Employees were fairly certain that their plant was going to be shut down and that many of them would either be laid off or relocated. Morale was not good, and people were less than enthusiastic to be attending a communications workshop.

I began the workshop with a series of exercises aimed at getting participants to bind and bond with one another. I must confess that I did not expect miracles, but the results amazed us all. One quiet, conservatively dressed woman with two kids related her adventures as a Harley Davidson biker and brought in pictures to show us. Another woman shared her passion for home craft projects and brought in a number of examples. Someone else revealed his hobby as an emergency ham radio operator. By the end of the workshop, people had discovered a wealth of stories and experiences in one another. These stories enabled them to see past their real and legitimate fears about the future.

SUMMARY

We have examined three facets of the story model:

Stories are used to	Stories have the following effects
Empower a speaker.	They entertain.
Create an environment.	They create trust and openness between yourself and others.
Bind and bond individuals.	They elicit stories from others.

Managers can try to inspire employees with motivational talks; or they can use stories to engage their audience, to induce reflection or as metaphors for problems to be solved. In doing the latter, they draw listeners in as collaborators and become more approachable.

Chapter 3

Stories Engage Our Minds in Active Listening and Allow Us to Negotiate Differences

STORIES ENGAGE OUR MINDS IN ACTIVE LISTENING

I was introduced to the concept of "active listening" by my father, Theodore, who is a conductor and composer. I love sitting by his side while he pores over an orchestra score. Of course, to me the notes on the page are little more than an abstraction. But to my father, they are a rich sea of sound and emotion. With his eyes, Theodore "hears" all of the instruments playing the music perfectly. He is quick to remind me that Beethoven wrote his Ninth Symphony when he was deaf. Theodore insists that not even the greatest recording of the Ninth Symphony can come close to what Beethoven must have heard in his head.

I remember watching my father conduct orchestra rehearsals. He begins his first rehearsal with any orchestra by saying, "If I cannot speak to you with this baton, we're both in trouble!" And while my father said very little, he communicated a lot, and he listened intently. Even during the loudest section of music, when all of the instruments are playing forte, my father can isolate the sound of one violinist playing the wrong sharp or flat. Communicating with one another would be a lot easier if we all had such exceptional listening skills.

Before we move away from music, take a moment to consider why the same piece of music evokes different emotions in different people. Could it be that the emotive power of music is tied to people's memories, stories, and the associations they make? In this respect, stories and music are very similar. Stories have multiple threads. Stories do not grow old. However, our imagination grows lazy. We need to challenge ourselves. Is it possible for us to find a new nugget of gold each time we hear or relay a story? Can we find an unturned rock, a new nuance? To do so, we must develop the capacity for active listening.

In the following story, the role of actively listening is related to leadership and the role it plays in seeing things from other people's perspectives:

Joe walked briskly to the auditorium. He loved teaching the MBA seminar on leadership. Today's topic was going to be tricky. How could he convey to the class the elusive concepts of active listening and empathy and their importance to leadership? As he made his way to the front of the room, he decided to tell them one of his favorite stories. When the class had settled into their seats, he began with these words.

"Once upon time there was a mighty king by the name of Stephan. Now Stephan had almost everything: land, wealth, and tremendous power. Sadly, Stephan was missing one thing: a wife. One day he turned to his chief advisor and said, 'You have the most beautiful daughter in the land. My life is complete, but I need a companion. I will marry your daughter. Go tell her my wishes. We must arrange a stupendous wedding feast as soon as possible.'

"The chief advisor went home in terror. He knew his daughter was very picky about the men she dated. What if she would not marry the king? The king would have his head for sure. Cautiously, the chief advisor approached his daughter Zalea and began his plea.

"'My dear Zalea, I have great news to share with you. The king wants to marry you. Isn't that wonderful?' Without pausing to take a breath or look into his daughter's eyes, he continued, 'I'll run back to the palace to tell the king you have accepted his proposal.'

"'Father, wait,' began Zalea. 'How could I possibly marry the king? I neither know nor love him. I am flattered by his proposal, but I cannot possibly accept it.'

"The chief advisor's face contorted with pain. 'Zalea, your poor father's head may be at stake here. You don't want to disappoint the king, do you? He is such a wonderful king and employer. Think of all the perks you will have as queen. I don't think it is a career opportunity you should pass up.'

"Zalea's face lit up. 'You're right, father. I know the king has a reputation as a good man, but he is young and lacks any marketable skills. Tell the king I will accept his proposal on one, and only one, condition.'

"The chief advisor's face relaxed. 'And what might that be?'

"Looking her father square in the eye, and with the autocratic tone of a queen, she said, 'The king must learn a trade. When he can demonstrate to me that he has a marketable skill, then I will accept his proposal.'

"The chief advisor's face became sullen. He recognized the tone of voice. His daughter had made up her mind and there would be no changing it. Slowly he walked back to the palace.

"Once there, the chief advisor did everything he could to avoid the king. Finally, the king tracked him down. 'Where have you been? I have been looking all over the palace for you. Tell me your daughter's decision.'

"'Well, Your Highness,' the chief advisor said, 'my daughter will gladly accept your proposal. However, she had one little request. Zalea wants you to learn a trade.'

"'A what?' roared the king.

"'A trade, Your Highness.' Fearing the worst, the chief advisor closed his eyes and pressed his hands together in prayer.

"'Hmm,' muttered the king. 'Chief advisor, I know now that your daughter is as wise as she is beautiful. I will fulfill her wish. Tomorrow I will begin to search for a trade to learn.'

"The chief advisor let out a huge sigh of relief and ran all the way home to tell his daughter the news.

"Over the next few days, the king observed and spoke to all sorts of craftsmen. He watched the marketing and advertising department haggle over product positioning and branding. He listened to overbearing sales pitches. He yawned uncontrollably as the bean counters in the accounting department verified his financial position, and he came close to losing his lunch as he listened to technologists in the information technology department frenetically espouse their e-commerce strategies. Finally, the king found an old weaver who began to show him the intricacies of his trade.

"The king worked at his loom night and day to learn his new trade. One day he called in his chief advisor to show him a splendid scarf he had woven. The scarf showed a red rose on a dark, forest-green background. The king asked his chief advisor to take the scarf to Zalea as a gift. When Zalea saw it she knew the king had learned the trade of weaving. Happily, she agreed to marry him, and there was a grand and joyous celebration.

"The king quickly learned that his wife was indeed very wise. He sought her advice on all the kingdom's affairs. One day he said to Zalea, 'I don't know what people in our kingdom want, or how they feel. I cannot rely on my advisors. They tell me what they think I want to hear. How can I learn to be sensitive to my people's needs?'

"'My dear,' Zalea began, 'you must walk in your people's shoes. Go to the market dressed as a common person. As you wander, listen to what people say to one another. Then I believe you will find answers to your questions.'

"So the king and some of his advisors disguised themselves and made their way to the market. As they strolled along, the king was amazed at what he learned. Around noon, the king turned to his advisors and said, 'I'm hungry. Lets get a bite to eat.'

"'Marvelous!' responded his chief advisor. 'Let's get out of these dingy clothes and head back to the palace for a proper meal.'

"'No,' the king retorted. 'I want to eat like the people in my kingdom. I overheard people talking about an excellent greasy spoon known for its burgers and Philly cheesesteak sandwiches. Let's go eat there.'

"The king led the way while his advisors sheepishly followed him. They arrived at the restaurant. As they tried to enter, a trap door opened beneath them and they fell into a deep, dark pit. Moments later the trap door opened and a hideous man snarled at them as he threw burgers down for them to eat. 'Now you know why I have the best burgers in the kingdom. My burgers are made from fat, plump people like you.' The man slammed the trap door shut and went away laughing.

"'What do we do now?' moaned one advisor.

"'We are as good as dead,' whimpered another.

"'Listen, Your Highness,' the chief advisor said, 'you'd better tell that idiot who we are. That will end this nonsense.'

"'Quiet, all of you!' yelled the king. 'If we tell this evil man who we are, we are as good as dead. Now, leave me alone for a moment. I need to think. None of you must utter a word the next time he comes.'

"A good deal later the trap door opened. 'Eat up, lads. I have lots of hungry customers to feed,' bellowed the evil man.

"'Excuse me, sir,' the king chimed in. 'I know you can't set us free, but my life is so precious to me. I can weave the most beautiful scarves you have ever seen. The queen at the palace pays great sums of money for them. Surely you realize that we can earn you more money by weaving scarves than you will earn from the measly burgers you can make from our bodies. If you give me a loom and some yarn, I will show you how I can make you a richer man.'

"'I'll think about it,' snorted the evil man. A few minutes later, the trap door opened and the evil man threw down a loom and some yarn for the king.

"The king worked all night. He wove a beautiful scarf with a red rose on a dark, forest-green background. In the morning he gave it to the evil man, saying, 'Take this scarf to Queen Zalea. She will pay you a handsome price for it.'

"The evil man ran all the way to the palace. The palace had been in total chaos since the king and his advisors had disappeared. When Zalea saw the scarf, she immediately recognized the work of her husband. She paid the evil man four pieces of gold and gave him stock options worth a good deal more. When the evil man left, Zalea had the king's army follow him.

"She herself rode at the head of the army. When they reached the evil man's restaurant, the army seized all his assets, instructed the Justice Department to break up his franchise, told the executioner to cut off his head, and freed the king and his advisors. And Zalea and the king rode off together into the sunset and lived happily ever after."

Analysis

King Stephan learns the value of active listening. When Zalea instructs the king to learn a trade before she will marry him, he recognizes Zalea's wisdom. He realizes that although he is a powerful king, he has no specific skills. So he goes on a fact-finding mission.

One of the joys of stories is that they evolve and adapt themselves to fit the audience to whom they are told. This story is being told to business school students, so our storyteller weaves in references and associations that will pique their interest.

The king discovers that there are many aspects of his kingdom and its people about which he knows nothing. He sets out on a discovery mission and decides to learn the art of weaving. Mastering any new skill requires time, patience, and a lot of active listening. The king is taking a vital first step toward better understanding his people. In many cultures, weavers are depicted as storytellers. By learning the art of weaving, the king is getting in touch with himself, his stories and, ultimately, his people.

Once the king and Zalea are married, he relies heavily on her for advice. He asks her a simple but profound question: What do his people think and feel? Zalea's response hits the heart of active listening. She tells the king, "You must walk in your people's shoes." Zalea is helping her husband develop compassion and empathy. When the king walks as a commoner among his people, he is amazed by what he hears and learns. The king succeeds in adopting a new frame of reference. He has effectively suspended his royal perspective and embraced the perspective of the people in his kingdom.

When we succeed in listening actively to each other's stories, and consider our own response to them, we enter into a new realm of understanding. We suddenly become capable of embracing contradictions and paradoxes. We become aware of competing thoughts, feelings, and emotions. And unlike the "rational mind," the "story mind" can entertain all of these possibilities without experiencing any dissonance.

Returning to the story, we see the king use his newfound wisdom and his trade when he and his advisors get caught by the evil man. The king does not use force. He knows neither force nor his social position will get him out of his predicament. Quite the contrary. The king must be cunning. In the end, it is the king's ability to listen actively that saves him and reunites him with his wise and beautiful wife.

Actively listening plays a critical role in verbal and written communications. The next story is about a memo. Behind the sound business recommendations of this memo, there is subtext.

Clyde read his memo one last time. As long as he was in control, he would do whatever it took to put Capital Success Training on the map. Since 1990, the company had contracted over 350 trainers to teach forty-five classes. During the last three years, Clyde had increased the company's revenues by 60 percent by introducing the sale of books, videos, and audiotapes during classes.

Leo sighed as he opened the memo from Capital Success Training. It was difficult to stay on top of all of the company's changes. Since Leo had started, he had learned how to be an effective salesman. At every class he taught, he set up a sales table in the back of the room to display the products Capital Success Training shipped to him. Leo was not fond of sales, but with the help of an assistant he usually managed to sell enough to make a decent commission. In a few minutes he was supposed to meet a group of Capital Success trainers for a drink. He reread the memo in the meantime. It read as follows:

FROM: Clyde Clawson

TO: Capital Success Trainers

SUBJECT: New Sales Policies

Everyone has been working very hard. As we continue to grow, I want to go over some new policies. Here is a summary of what we need to do:

1. Tighten up the product list of books, tapes, and audiotapes sold at our classes.

2. Review which classes to ship products to.

3. Eliminate sales–administrative assistants for classes with low attendance.

4. Evaluate trainers based on their class evaluations and sales results.

To some of you, these changes may sound drastic, unfair, arbitrary, demeaning, punitive, or pick the complaining adjective of your choice. You're entitled to your own opinion, of course, but make sure you understand and consider the facts before you jump to conclusions.

We are financially solid, and our market share continues to grow. Those of you who watch our competition know they've been declining in number of classes presented, number of employees, and number of trainers contracted. We continue to grow in all categories.

We believe we'll stay ahead of the pack by making proactive, smart business decisions before economic or market conditions force us to make reactive, defensive ones. As long as we can protect and nurture the best features of our business by culling the worst, we're going to remain healthy.

How all of this might impact you personally is up to you. If you're thinking, "Hey, my sales are always good, so I won't see much change," you're right. Or if you're thinking, "Well, I can learn how to sell out of the catalog as long as I've got samples to show," you're right, too, and you'll probably get your sales back up to the point where shipping isn't a question! But if your reaction is, "They won't buy anything if they can't take it with them," I'd guess you're one of the trainers who hasn't sold much of anything under any conditions. If that continues to be a convenient excuse, I'll miss working with you.

Once the urge to call and play the "ain't it awful" game with your best trainer friend or most insightful assistant has passed, please call me. I've got lots of great ideas on how we all can prosper from product sales!

As our business evolves and grows to meet the demands of the marketplace, change is inevitable. We make little adjustments all the time, as you know, because that's the kind of quick-response management that allows us to stay strong and keep growing. To make sure we're always moving forward, always giving our customers what they want, and always providing trainers with opportunities to train and always operating as cost-effectively as possible, some conditions demand more extensive change:

1. Trainers with the best sales results will be scheduled to teach workshops first.

2. We'll ship products to your classes when your sales history on that topic and the projected attendance for that class indicate that your effort will generate enough sales to at least cover costs. Some classes will not have products shipped to them.

3. Every class and every trainer will get product catalogs, along with all the support we can muster to help everyone sell well. As your sales improve, so will your chances of having products shipped.

4. We're designing training programs to help you learn new techniques for selling from display samples and catalogs. You remain eligible to earn the established commission rates for each class, regardless of whether products are in the room.

5. For all classes where you will be acting as your own program manager, we will pay you an additional commission of 2 percent on the day's sales. And yes, in response to several of you who've asked, you may, with our advance approval, choose to be your own assistant in a high-attendance class when we can be assured customer service won't be sacrificed.

To be very frank, the better your sales record, the fewer changes you'll experience. Even for training topics where we normally wouldn't ship product, you'll still have every opportunity to prove that your sales performance warrants our going to the expense of doing so. We both benefit when you're successful at product sales.

Trainers who've been achieving excellent sales results will see very little, if any, change as a result of these new procedures. Trainers who've been struggling with sales but working with us to improve will be supported as long as they're making progress with sales that pay their way. Trainers who don't produce acceptable sales results, who don't demonstrate any effort, or who just don't care will find that we will match their level. They certainly won't get any products at their classes and if their inability to produce any sales persists, they may find that our ability to schedule them for classes has ended.

We are working on a variety of programs to help you boost your sales.

A final note: Please don't become the victim of rumor or gossip. As trees grow, they need to be pruned so that dead wood doesn't slow the advance of strong branches and leaves. That's exactly what, and only what, we're doing. Tree branches, however, don't have the luxury of choosing their own destiny. You do. When you need more explanation or have questions, ask me. Let's work hard together to keep our growth going.

Leo folded the memo in half and stuck it in his pocket. He wondered what the other trainers would say about Clyde's memo. He was sure there must be another story here. Leo shrugged his shoulders, put on his coat, and headed out for a much-needed drink.

Analysis

In order to penetrate to the heart of Clyde's memo, we must look for the subtext. Clyde is on a mission. From one perspective, his memo appears reasonable. Capital Success Training is making sound business decisions. Clyde is introducing policies to reduce costs and increase profits. Who could argue with that?

But take a look at the tone of Clyde's memo. Is it persuasive or domineering? If you were a trainer reading the memo, would you be angry and feel insulted by his tone? Clyde does not leave room for the trainers' reactions. He tries to anticipate their emotions and responds by slinging threats at them:

> Now to some of you, these changes may sound drastic, unfair, arbitrary, demeaning, punitive, or pick the complaining adjective of your choice. . . . But if your reaction is, "They won't buy anything if they can't take it with them," I'd guess you're one of the trainers who hasn't been able or willing to sell much of anything under any conditions. If that continues to be a convenient excuse, I'll miss working with you. . . . Once the urge to call and play the "ain't it awful" game with your best trainer friend or most insightful assistant has passed, please call me.

Clyde is a frightened bully. His story is out of control. Even his use of a tree metaphor is out of place:

> A final note: Please don't become the victim of rumor or gossip. As trees grow, they need to be pruned so that dead wood doesn't slow the advance of strong branches and leaves. That's exactly what, and only what, we're doing. Tree branches, however, don't have the luxury of choosing their own destiny. You do.

There could be a million stories behind Clyde's tone. Perhaps his boss is breathing down his neck to achieve better sales and profits. Clyde may believe his job is at stake if he doesn't fatten the bottom line through sales.

One thing we can be sure of is that Clyde has lost his perspective and control. And while his tone and his failure to motivate trainers may be clear to us, Clyde himself is oblivious to all of the subtexts of his message. Clyde is locked into his story. Our capacity to actively listen to his story lets us gain insights, but Clyde's inability to listen holds him prisoner.

Incidentally, Clyde's memo sheds light on Capital Success Training's story. What business are they really in? From the memo it appears that Capital Success is more interested in selling products than providing training. Maybe it's time for them to rename their company Capital Success Resources and Lectures.

NEGOTIATE DIFFERENCES

Conflicts in organizations are the result of clashing points of view. Of course people have different points of view, but consider some of the dichotomies that naturally exist in organizations. For example, there is usually competition between sales and marketing, product development and marketing, or tensions between labor and management. Each functional area has its own organizational perspective and its own turf to protect. Often the interests of management are not in sync with the desires and needs of labor. Managers are challenged to leverage each perspective while negotiating the differences between them.

When negotiating differences in either a conflict or decision-making process, it is essential to hear, appreciate, understand, and acknowledge all of the perspectives. It turns out that stories are the quickest way to gain important insights. We are inclined to rationally explain and justify our perspectives; however, there are always experiences, values, and beliefs behind perspectives. Stories shed light on these things and can reveal a whole host of hard-to-identify motivations, like fears and self-interests. Stories get to the heart of matters and help us imagine other perspectives.

What's inherently difficult about negotiating differences is that when faced with two strong points of views, opinions, or ideas, there is always some validity to each of them. This can be paralyzing. If each point of view has some validity, how do you draw a fair conclusion? Think about how a trial works. Each side presents its story. A jury has to work through each side of the story. In the end, they synthesize all of the information and formulate a story of their own to make a decision.

Using stories as a way of negotiating differences or getting to the root cause of a problem works because, unlike reasoning, stories are not linear in nature. While the sequence of events in a story follows a logical order, the themes and messages contained in it allow our minds to entertain paradoxes. Through stories we can simultaneously hold multiple and conflicting points of view as being true and consider them all without one negating the other. This leads to a very rich experience, since our minds must open to a whole world of nuances.

SUMMARY

We have examined two more facets of the story model:

Stories are used to	Stories have the following effects
Engage our minds in active listening.	Listen actively in order to
	—Understand context and perspective.
	—Identify the root cause of a problem.
	—Uncover resistance and hidden agendas.
	Shift perspectives in order to
	—See each other.
	—Experience empathy.
	—Enter new frames of reference.
Negotiate differences.	Hold diverse points of view.
	Become aware of operating biases and values.

Through active listening, managers can quickly get to the bottom of situations, discover the root cause of problems, and honestly assess their biases. Effective leaders know how to enter new frames of reference in order to see things from other people's perspectives. Stories also allow them to hold diverse points of view and negotiate differences without abnegating their own.

Chapter 4

Stories Encode Information, Are Tools for Thinking, Serve as Weapons, Bring about Healing

STORIES ENCODE INFORMATION

Company X's first quarter results for 1999 were in, and the final numbers were staggering. Janice Shaker, president and CEO of the company, was sitting at her desk reading a slew of congratulatory e-mails from members of the board of directors when John Moore, vice president of manufacturing, came bursting into her office.

"I really don't know what to do, Janice," he began. "I have tried everything I can think of but nothing seems to be working. For the past three months, the number of defective products shipped and returned to us has been increasing. Let me give you an idea of the scope of this problem: Last month, 20 percent of our products shipped were returned for a refund. I met with the folks in manufacturing to see if whether they had any ideas or required any help. They believed the root of the problem was sloppy and careless work by the team of quality control engineers.

"I met with Tim Jenkins, the director of quality control, and he assured me he would have a little talk with his team of engineers. One month later, things have only gotten worse. I heard through the grapevine that Tim threatened to fire his manager of quality control if things did not improve."

Janice took a moment to think. Then she smiled to herself and said to John, "Thanks for the heads up. I'll take it from here. Oh, by the way, be sure to clear next Tuesday on your calendar for a luncheon with all of manufacturing to celebrate our record-breaking quarter."

Janice watched John walk out of her office shaking his head. She sighed to herself and closed all of the open e-mail messages from the board of directors and quickly wrote the following memo:

FROM: Janice Shaker

TO: ·   All Employees of Manufacturing/Quality Control

SUBJECT: Luncheon

Our results from the last quarter are in and I am proud to inform you that all of your hard work and dedication has paid off. We exceeded everyone's expectations. I think we all deserve an opportunity to celebrate a little. On Tuesday, all manufacturing will stop at 1:00 PM for the day. We will have a specially catered luncheon. At 3:00 PM, everyone will be free to go home early. I am attaching a menu; please return your selections to my office by 4:00 PM Friday.

Looking forward to seeing and speaking with you then.

Janice called in her assistant, Chris. "Chris, would you please ask Sea Point Catering to cater a 1:00 PM luncheon for us on Tuesday. When you get them on the phone, please buzz me; I need to go over a few things with them."

It didn't take people long to return their menus. Everyone was eagerly awaiting delicacies like lobster diavolo, haddock stuffed with king crab legs and shrimp, and soft shell crabs, to name just a few.

At 1:15 PM on Tuesday, Janice walked into the reception hall. Chris and John ran up to her in a panic. John blurted, "You'd better have a word with the caterers. No one has the food they ordered. Every single order is wrong. How could these people be so incompetent?"

Janice brushed past them and walked toward the podium. She observed people frantically swapping plates in an attempt to get the dish they had ordered. Silence fell upon the room as Janice began to speak. "Good afternoon, everyone. Let's all dig in and enjoy our scrumptious lunches from Sea Point Catering." Before Janice could continue, she heard Tim Jenkins mutter, "We would if we had the food we ordered." Janice focused her eyes on Tim and slowly issued the following request, "Will Sea Point Catering please serve everyone their meal according to the second seating plan I faxed you."

In less than five minutes everyone had exactly what he had ordered. When Janice spoke during dessert, she thanked and congratulated everyone for all of the hard work. She shared her vision for the next quarter, emphasizing the critical role of making their customers happy by ensuring the highest-quality product. Janice concluded by apologizing on behalf of Sea Point Catering. She claimed full responsibility for the mix-up, since she had faxed them two different seating plans.

At the end of the luncheon, John walked up to Janice wearing a sheepish grin and said, "You did that on purpose, didn't you? Well, whether you did or not, Tim definitely benefited from the experience. I heard him and his manager strategizing with their team of engineers on ways to improve quality control."

Janice just smiled. Maybe now she could get back to responding to some of those glowing e-mails.

Analysis

Stories are efficient encoders of information. One perfect example of this is stories from different cultural, religious, or mystical traditions. In these stories, lessons or meanings are never spelled out. Instead, you are invited to connect to a story or experience through active listening, to unravel its significance and generate your own meaning. In this way, stories are also fluid. As you return to your stories and memories, new nuances, insights, and shades of meaning emerge.

In this story, Janice concluded that Tim's efforts to impress upon his team of engineers the impact of poor quality control and his attempts to motivate his manager with threats are ineffectual. She realized that she must find a more dramatic way than Tim's traditional approach to make the point. Janice decides to model the frustrating result of an experience with bad quality control by having everyone's lunch order purposely messed up.

Janice used her imagination to conjure up a scenario. She created the situation she needed in order to encode her message. Her story thinking led her to construct an experience that stimulated the imagination of Tim and his team. Janice, being a true leader, guided Tim toward a creative solution to the problem. He and his team are not likely to forget Sea Point Catering's luncheon. Janice not only succeeded in addressing the quality control problems, but she also created a story that will inevitably become part of the company's culture.

STORIES AS TOOLS FOR THINKING

Stories equip our minds with templates for thinking. We can use stories to describe one thing in terms of another. New concepts are not abstract if we use stories or analogies that resonate with a person's knowledge and experience. For example, I remember teaching a class on technical writing. Many students struggled with writing clear and succinct explanations, so I had them take a technical concept and explain it using an analogy a teenager could understand. The hard part was thinking of an analogy or metaphor that applied to the concept. The rest was straightforward. They were amazed at how easy the concept was to explain and how simple it became once they found an analogy.

Stories are particularly effective thinking tools when the imagery is distinctive. Take the following short phrase and the story behind it: "Canary in a coal mine."

The contrast of a bright yellow canary with a dark coal mine is a striking image. Miners in coal mines used to carry a canary in a cage on their shoulders. If the canary died, they knew the air in the mine was not safe.

A leader might use the image of a canary in a coal mine with a group of managers tasked with a potentially disastrous project. Undoubtedly the team feels uneasy. They may even believe that the business is setting them up for failure. Emotions left unexpressed can hamper objective decision making. However, the image of the canary does not need to be negative. Story thinking enables us to validate emotions and articulate possibilities. A leader can guide his or her team from negative emotions of fear and resentment about being set up for failure to positive ones of excitement about the challenge that lies ahead of them. The story can be rewritten. Why not give the story a new spin? The canary neither has to die or be stuck in a cage. Build upon the story. Point out that unlike canaries, the team is free to make choices to avoid disaster. Show how the team will be brave pioneers for the business.

Learning results from piecing together our experiences. One experience builds on another. We are pattern recognition machines. Studies done on chess players have shown that one of the major differences between novice and expert players is that experts, faced with a novel board position, draw upon previous games with similar positions to select the best move. Experts have more experience; and whether they realize it or not, they apply that experience to novel situations.

I remember hearing an anecdote about a famous teacher. His students challenged him to tell them what lessons they could learn from catching a train or sending a telegram. He replied, "A train teaches us that even a second can make a difference, and a telegram teaches us to measure all of our words because every one of them counts." This demonstrates the flexibility and applicability of stories as tools for thinking and reflection. The act of catching a train or sending a telegram is not intrinsically loaded with meaning. Thinking "analogically" produces a unique twist.

Case studies are another example of story thinking. They are marvelous teaching tools and generate lots of great discussions. Case studies replace the abstractions of business theory with story. They also broaden the learning process. Previously read case studies can be related to the one currently being discussed.

Stories are wonderful thinking tools. Through stories we reflect on our experiences. Experiences mean nothing if we don't learn anything from them. Stories bring the past viscerally alive to our minds. When we retell a story, our mind relives the experience. Each rewinding of our mental tape recorder is an opportunity to gain new insights.

We all have lots of experiences and therefore lots of stories. To put a twist on Plato's saying: "The unexamined story is not worth having."

STORIES SERVE AS WEAPONS

Like anything else, stories are neutral. How we use them determines their impact. Stories can be used in destructive and aggressive ways. For example, they can be purposely misleading. In some contexts when the word story is used, it implies that the speaker is lying. Perhaps someone is telling a tall tale or simply misconstruing facts to influence the listener in a negative way. Either way stories are being consciously used as weapons.

Stories can be very convincing. Think about how stories were used to fuel the Cold War. The Communists ran a propaganda machine. Exaggerations and outright lies were constructed to glorify Communism and portray the United States as a villain. Likewise, the United States was just as guilty of using stories to promote fear of Communism. In these examples stories are used to manipulate people's thoughts and feelings.

Character attacks in political campaigns are another example of how stories can be used to manipulate people's thoughts and feelings. Although character attacks are perceived as being negative, campaign strategists resort to them because they are so effective. These attacks involve telling stories that cast the opposing candidate in a negative light. Once a story is told it is likely to stick in people's minds. After the fact candidates apologize and retreat from character assassinations, but it doesn't really matter because the stories told have already had their effect.

In a legal or business setting, stories are used to support arguments and make convincing cases. Viewed in this way, the presentation and interpretation of statistical data is a form of storytelling and is used all the time to support people's agendas. Look at Wall Street. The analysis of a company's financials and performance indicators has been known to dramatically affect the valuation of a company. Most of the time these valuations are fair, but there have been times when people have used data to tell a story that misrepresents a company.

The stronger your stories are, the more convincing you will be. We've all been victims of "buying" or believing a story that turns out to be a tool for furthering someone else's agenda. Taken to an extreme, this is what con artists do. They are capable of painting such a powerful picture that we become easily swayed. Con artists and pathological liars frequently succeed in manipulating us because they make us believe their stories.

Stories are powerful. Since they are the way our minds work, they can be used for self-serving goals. Your gut instinct is the best defense and warning system you have against stories used as weapons. On the surface it can be hard to detect manipulative stories. If you pay attention to cues, such as the context in which the story is used and the possible motivations someone may have for telling a story, and note that other stories conflict with the one you are being told, then you stand a better chance of avoiding deception. If we can help it, we do not want to be swept away by a false story; therefore, sometimes, as in the story *The Emperor's New Clothes*, we may even have to stand up against common opinion to dispel a myth.

STORIES BRING ABOUT HEALING

Stories stimulate our imagination. Significant healing can occur through stories. For example, many schools of therapy incorporate narratives or storytelling as a key part of the healing process. Individuals work through their past or current issues by speaking about their experiences. Healing occurs when individuals realize they are not locked into behavior, thoughts, feelings, self-perceptions, or beliefs reflected in their stories. By working through their stories and gaining insights, they can begin to envision new possibilities.

The right story told at the right time can help another person. Remember the story of Michael Moore, the CEO, and Jerry Johnson, the mail clerk. Recognizing that Jerry was struggling with his job, Michael shared his experience of how badly he bungled his first job as a telephone operator. Michael's story allows Jerry to rewrite his own. Left to his own perceptions, Jerry is likely to believe he is incapable of climbing the corporate ladder if he cannot even deliver mail. Michael's story is liberating and healing.

Sharing stories promotes healing when there is tension or conflict. Through active listening we can hear another perspective. Misunderstandings and breakdowns in communications are overcome. Healing becomes possible when we are willing to embrace other perspectives. Stories are the most efficient way of communicating these perspectives and catalyzing healing.

SUMMARY

We have examined the last four facets of the story model:

Stories are used to	Stories have the following effects
Encode information.	Create a working metaphor to illuminate an opinion, rationale, vision, or decision.
Act as tools for thinking.	Establish connections between different ideas and concepts to
Serve as weapons.	support an opinion or decision.
Bring about healing.	Think outside the box to generate creative solutions and breakthroughs.

Stories can contain so much information. If a picture is worth a thousand words, a story must be worth a hundred thousand words. Thinking with stories enables us to process a lot of information at the same time. Lengthy and logical reasoning processes are accelerated with story thinking. In addition, we can work with multiple stories and perspectives simultaneously even if they contradict each other. Since stories are the way our minds work, we can use them either as weapons or to promote healing.

See Appendix B for a summary of the story model and Chapters 2 through 4.

PART II

Putting Stories to Work
in Human Resources,
Training, and
Organizational Development

Chapter 5

The Role Stories Can Play
in Human Resources

This chapter looks at some of the ways stories can be put to work in human resources. Collecting and analyzing stories from your organization makes it easier to perform the following tasks:

1. Recruiting
2. Interviewing
3. Employee orientation
4. Performance appraisals
5. Employee relations
6. Conflict resolution

In this chapter we briefly explore each of these areas. The remaining four chapters in this section offer a comprehensive strategy for using stories in the areas of training, competency modeling, knowledge management, corporate culture, change management, and leadership.

RECRUITING

Companies are hungry for talented employees. To attract and retain talent, companies offer all sorts of incentives and benefits. Many companies have had to learn the hard way that it costs more to continually hire and train new employees than to find the right ones and retain them. Recruiting should be more than a numbers game. It needs to be a matter of excellent communication, and one of the best ways of establishing that is through storytelling.

The Internet has given recruiters new tools for reaching larger pools of applicants more quickly than ever before. Yet they still have problems finding the right people. Leaving supply and demand aside, let's look at how companies can use stories to improve their odds of attracting candidates.

Stories are the perfect way to bring a company and a job to life for a prospective employee. Your challenge is to bring the company and job alive for a candidate. Granted, it is easier to tell someone facts and figures about a company or read them a job description, but that is flat and ineffective. Put on your competitor's hat and differentiate your company.

It all begins with active listening. Start by trying to elicit stories from an applicant. Here are some questions to ask to get the ball rolling:

1. What does the applicant know about the company?
2. What has he or she heard about it from other people?
3. Has the applicant read any recent articles about the company?
4. Why is the applicant interested in the company?
5. How does the applicant envision his or her position at the company?
6. Has the applicant explored the company's website? If so, what did he or she learn?
7. How would the candidate present the company to someone else?
8. Has the applicant heard stories from other employees?

Let candidates' stories and assumptions about the company drive your conversations. Use their stories to figure out what stories you should tell. Scan their stories for accurate facts and impressions versus gossip. Evaluate their choice of story and tone for things like

1. Underlying attitude toward the company
2. Attitude toward work in general
3. Level of interest
4. Communication style

If you have positive feelings about the candidate, share a story that will spark his or her imagination. How about a success story of an employee? Perhaps you can whet his or her appetite by telling a story of how someone in the role you are recruiting for had a profound impact on the company or a customer.

Would an advertiser just list product features and expect customers to come running? Not likely. Successful ads grab our attention and somehow personally connect us to the product or service involved. Initially, you will find it much harder to think and communicate in terms of stories, but it gets easier with practice. Before you know it you will have collected a wealth of stories about the company, and you will get very good at listening to the stories candidates tell. Stories are not for the "faint of imagination or passion." If you do not believe in the company you are recruiting for, your job is going to be difficult, and if you take the time to be aware of your own stories, you will notice that you cannot hide your true thoughts and feelings. They will show through in the stories you tell, or in their absence.

Work with your company's public relations or communications department to incorporate stories in all of your recruiting strategies:

1. Newspaper ads
2. Radio and television ads
3. Job fair displays
4. Brochures
5. Web sites

And remember: Stories do not need to be long, only effective.

INTERVIEWING

Before you even speak to a candidate, *really* read his or her resume with your "story mind." Some recruiters do not even glance at a resume. Don't waste your own and your candidates' time by having them reiterate information that can be easily learned by reading the resume. Instead of making a candidate feel important and comfortable, demonstrating you haven't read the resume will have the opposite effect. The more comfortable the candidate is, the easier it will be to elicit stories.

As you read a resume, look beyond the list of dates, degrees, and facts. In addition, temporarily set aside your laundry list of requirements. Now is the time to activate your imagination. Use the information before you to construct a story and image of the person. Synthesize the details to generate preliminary impressions.

Consider exploring the following areas in addition to asking your standard questions:

1. Do you see any patterns in the candidate's job history?
2. What is the most intriguing piece of information?

3. What experience on the resume is the least relevant to the job the candidate is interviewing for?
4. Why does the candidate enjoy this type of work?
5. What is his or her motivation?

For example, let's pretend you are trying to staff a research position for your legal department. An example of part of a candidate's resume is shown in Figure 5.1.

On the surface, this resume (Figure 5.1) appears to be dry and straightforward. Hidden in the details, however, are dozens of interesting stories. Each story can provide a wealth of insight. For example:

Guiding Question	Relevant Information	Interviewer's Story Prompt	Points to Explore
Do you see any patterns in the candidate's job history?	Housing	Tell me about the most memorable housing case you worked on.	Does the candidate take pride in any aspect of the case? Does the story shed any light on candidate's approach to things or values?
What is the most intriguing piece of information?	Researched and drafted legal memoranda on federal housing tax credits, low-income housing development, compliance issues, architectural access, fair housing, federal, state, and local historic sites.	If you could rewrite any of the federal housing laws, which ones would you choose? How would you change them? Can you give me examples of cases you worked on that guide your current thinking?	How does the candidate form an opinion? Are there issues the candidate is passionate about?
What experience listed on the resume is the least relevant to the job he or she is interviewing for?	Activities: Participant, Some University Summer Institute of Law, exotic foreign country	Tell me about your summer. What was it like to live in an exotic foreign country? How is that country's legal system different from ours?	How does the candidate handle cultural differences? How might the culture and work environment of your organization affect the candidate?

Figure 5.1
Sample Resume

EXPERIENCE Sample & Sample, Inc. Nowhere, USA
            ASSOCIATE   *Time Fiction to Time Fiction*

- Experience in residential and commercial conveyancing, commercial lending, condominium conversion, business and corporate law, estates, wills and trusts.
- Draft estate instruments including wills and trusts.
- Advise clients on estate instruments suitable for clients' estate planning goals.
- Represent major banking institutions in residential and commercial lending.
- Conduct commercial and residential loan closings. Advise clients as to title issues.
- Manage client and vendor relationships.
- Negotiate, prepare, and review loan documents for commercial loan closings and documentation for organizing, incorporating and amending some State for-profit and non-profit organizations.

Independent Contractor Nowhere, USA *Time Fiction to Time Fiction*

- Legal research and writing on various topics for several general practice firms.
- Researched, drafted, and reviewed environmental and zoning opinions, documentation necessary to obtain federal housing tax credits in low-income housing development, and various documentation for organizing and incorporating not-for-profit tenant associations.
- Researched and drafted legal memoranda on issues of federal housing tax credits, low-income housing development, compliance issues, architectural access, fair housing, federal, state and local historic sites, nonconforming zoning and land uses, and contract issues arising in low-income housing development.

EDUCATION   Some Law School Juris Doctor
            Activities
            Participant, Some University Summer Institute of Law, Exotic Foreign Country

Interviewing should be fun. Go beyond the demands of filling jobs, and see each candidate as a story waiting to unfold. Some people find it easy to look for stories in a candidate's resume and ask the right questions to elicit them. If it is not immediately easy for you, there is no need to worry. Start with the desire to discover candidates, and with a little practice, the rest will become second nature.

EMPLOYEE ORIENTATION

How do things look from the perspective of a new employee? What do you want him or her to know about your company, and what do you want him or her to know about the job? Time spent on employee orientation can be organized into the following types of activities:

- Structured–formal
- Informational
- Unstructured
- Coaching–informal

Structured–Formal

This is your chance to formally welcome an employee to your company. Think of it as a ritual. People appreciate ceremony, and all of us want to feel that we are getting special attention. Ask senior-level managers to host a breakfast or lunch for new employees. Use it to share a vision of the company, celebrate the company's success stories, and introduce employees to the company's defining stories. Coach the managers on how to use stories. Select stories that will create an environment full of energy and possibilities—for example, the story of how the company got started. Managers should share personal stories about their involvement and experience with the company.

The formal orientation should include time and activities that encourage new employees to use stories to dialogue with one another and with senior employees and to start the process of binding and bonding. One way of doing this is to place cue cards with story prompts at everyone's seat. Some suitable story prompts are:

- My first job
- The day I grew up and figured out what I wanted to be
- The funniest thing that ever happened to me at work
- A fun fact about myself

- My greatest success
- My favorite hero or heroine

Such an orientation will leave new employees feeling as if they belong.

Informational Time

New employees have to digest a lot of information. What is the most efficient way? A nonlinear approach is best. If you have a room full of people, and everyone has to listen to the same presentation, you are slowing down many people. A speaker offers one stream of information, yet everyone assimilates information at his or her own rate. Our minds tend to wander. Allow each person to follow his or her own path of questions and needs.

Use technology to your advantage. Set up an Intranet site. Employees can use their web browser to read policies, sign documents, enroll in plans, and get answers to questions. However, it's very important that you do not eliminate anyone's access to a human resources professional. Many employees will want to speak directly with someone. They may not feel comfortable having their questions answered through an Intranet site. Technology is not an excuse to lose your focus on internal customer service. How employees perceive your treatment of them directly affects your company's bottom line.

An Intranet is also a perfect vehicle for maintaining an employee orientation process for all of your employees. Groupware, collaboration, and knowledge management software packages are in vogue. Many technology companies are scrambling to develop tools for capturing and presenting knowledge and making it searchable. Collecting, storing, and mining information is not enough. Companies want to transform their information into knowledge. One of the principal enablers is story. Use stories to express your company's best practices and lessons learned. Employees from one area of the company will benefit from hearing other employees' experiences. In this way, an Intranet site can be a way of maintaining an ongoing orientation for all of your employees.

Unstructured Time

Part of any new employee's orientation includes meeting lots of people. Put together a list of all the people he or she should meet, and indicate the reason for each choice and what you hope for from each conversation. This list should include an indication of why you want the new employee to meet each person and what you hope will be gained from each conversation. You must also take the time to speak with the people on your list. Give them a sense of what you want them to discuss, and ask them to share as much as they possibly can in the form of stories. Help them to think of some useful stories to recount. Here are some options:

1. Customer interactions
2. Successful projects
3. Lessons learned
4. Department history
5. Personal history
6. Challenges ahead

To emphasize the importance of stories as the principal learning and communication vehicle, let me use the analogy of acquiring a new skill. When you learned how to ride a bicycle, drive a car, or learn a sport, all of the verbal instructions in the world did not help until you physically experienced the sensations. It's just as difficult to be a new employee. A new employee will not be lacking for verbal instructions. What he or she needs are stories to activate the imagination. Stories are like physical sensations. Of course, a new employee's best teachers will be his or her experiences. However, before an employee begins to acquire experiences, hearing stories will make him or her more aware of what to pay attention to and learn.

Coaching–Informal Time

Part of any employee's continuing orientation must include coaching. The coach needs to take the time to build a relationship with the new employee. Trust and respect are the key ingredients. Without them, coaching is perceived negatively. Stories will help you build rapport, share knowledge, and assess what areas of knowledge and performance need attention.

PERFORMANCE APPRAISALS

If you dread performance appraisals and they feel like a formal requirement devoid of meaning, you are not alone—but what a shame. Performance appraisals can be a great process for giving feedback, rewarding performance, improving performance, and conducting strategic planning. Unfortunately, we have become slaves to the bureaucracies we have created and are paralyzed by the organizational and political ramifications of evaluating employees' performances. Stories can come to our rescue.

Although appraisals include space for comments, we are more focused on quantifying an employee's performance:

Employee demonstrates ability to follow through on all his or her assignments.

1	2	3	4	5

Strongly disagree   Strongly agree

There is more to be learned from the stories driving a perception than from the quantitative rating. For example, a manager may give an employee a low evaluation. What if an employee on one or two important occasions purposely dropped the ball on an assignment? What if his plate had been too full, and he prioritized his projects? In the absence of any formal instructions, what if he then dropped what he was doing so he could focus on what he thought was a mission-critical project? What if he was right? What if by doing so he saved the company money? There are many "what ifs" here. The point is that the supervisor filling out the evaluation or conducting the performance review may be totally unaware of the stories.

Stories provide a mechanism for dialoguing. There is a wealth of information to be learned. Appraisals should be viewed as a two-way street. How does an employee's performance reflect upon the company? Are there things the company needs to do better? Does the company need to provide more resources or more information? How can the company strategically align its objectives with the performance goals of its employees?

Elicit stories from employees. Listen carefully to their explanations. What were the causes of their successes? Why did they perform below expectations in another area? Get them to use stories to envision new performance goals and devise tactics for achieving them.

Take the time to revisit your performance appraisal process and tools. If you are not careful, you may inadvertently discourage an employee. Be sure to define and clarify future expectations. Deemphasize quantifying performance, and incorporate stories to promote dialogue and learning.

CONFLICT RESOLUTION

One of the main causes of conflict is a breakdown of communication. Communication always breaks down when we cannot see another person's perspective. Understanding another person's point of view means we must often suspend our own. We do not like to abandon our perspective. Doing so can be very disorienting. So, entering into a conflict actually becomes the path of least resistance. It does not take much energy to start a conflict. Yet ironically, holding on to negative feelings takes more energy than resolving a conflict. Even negative perception drives future destructive behavior, and things can quickly spiral out of control.

Let's use a simple example. Joe Employee and Jane Manager are having problems. Joe is furious with Jane because she will not give him funds to hire an outside consultant to help with a project. Initially, Jane had promised him all of the resources he would need. The project was a top priority. Jane had selected Joe to head it up because of his proven ability to deliver. Jane had also recognized that outside help would be necessary in order to complete the project. Joe took on the project in good faith, understanding he would be able to hire consultants. When things suddenly changed, and Joe could not hire outside consultants, he took it personally. He believes Jane is setting him up for failure. Joe starts going out of his way to criticize Jane and lets other projects slip through the cracks.

Due to new management, Jane's budget was cut by more than 30 percent in the middle of the year. New priorities are being articulated, and management has been unclear about its new direction. Jane is experiencing a lot of pressure and uncertainty. She is doing her best to get through all the chaos. She is frustrated that Joe, one of her best and most loyal employees, is being cantankerous. Jane is cross with him at meetings, and starts to cut back on other resources Joe needs.

Your job is to be a story facilitator. Joe and Jane need to tell their stories. You need to get behind each story and help the two see each other's perspective. Active listening will play a major role. Joe needs to see how he became wrapped up in the project and inattentive to Jane and her situation. He will have to recognize how his zeal for the project affected his behavior and attitude. Perhaps Jane had always been a good communicator, but the current pressures made it difficult for her. She may also have been waiting for clearer information from powers above. Jane will need to see how seriously Joe has taken the project, and how disillusioned he became when he was unable to complete it. Despite the lack of information, and the company's conservative management style, Jane needs to acknowledge the impact of her poor communication.

Before conflicts happen, offer employees workshops on how to resolve their conflicts by actively listening to each other's stories. Try conducting conflict resolutions in a special room. Decorate the room with pictures and objects that remind people of the company's big picture and their experiences in the workshop. Encourage employees to use the special room before a conflict escalates to the point where a facilitator is required. The goal is not to eliminate conflicts but to seize them as opportunities for increasing knowledge and encouraging richer communication.

SUMMARY

Maintaining good communication with employees from the time they are recruited and throughout their entire tenure with the company is central to human resources. We have taken a brief look at some of the ways stories can be used to improve communication. Being conscious of using stories and putting them to work for you may take some practice but the benefits are great. Stories will work well for human resources because they represent the way our mind works and are the most efficient form of communication.

Chapter 6

Using Stories in Training

Stories used in training improve communication and accelerate learning. Effective trainers and facilitators use stories. After I greet a group, the first words out of my mouth are a story. Sometimes it's a simple icebreaker:

> Good morning! I had a chance to meet many of you as you came in this morning. Does anyone remember my name? Yes, that's right, it's Terrence Gargiulo *(as I write my name on a flip chart)*. On my birth certificate my name is Terenzio. Do you remember playing the game Red Rover as a child? Two teams line up on opposite ends of a field and everyone holds hands to create a human chain-link fence. Imagine a team of children yelling, "Red Rover, Red Rover, send *(and I pause and gesture for them to say my name)* Terenzio on over." I pause again. It just wasn't going to work, so I go by Terrence. Feel free to call me "Terenzio," "Terrence," "Hey you," or whatever works.

This example works on different levels. For starters, it gets people to laugh. I want people to know that we are going to have fun together. If any of us take ourselves or the class too seriously, we aren't going to learn much. Second, it allows me to immediately be personable and vulnerable with the group. If I am going to ask them to share their thoughts and feelings during a class, I need to set the stage. This quick story serves to integrate me into the group.

Notice how the second sentence out of my mouth is a question. Right from the start I want to establish a pattern of participation and dialogue. I ask participants to imagine a common childhood game to momentarily move their thoughts away from all the things they are thinking about. The story activates their imaginations and prepares them to consider new perspectives and thereby learn.

Little has changed in how companies design and deliver training. Why do we think catchy slides and thick binders of course materials make an excellent course? Although stories are the way the mind works, much of our formal education does not promote or develop our innate capacity. It's a new paradigm for most people. Any training we design should include stories as a core part of its method. Approached in this way, training becomes unpredictable but extremely powerful. Relegate informational or didactic training to self-paced delivery mechanisms such as Web-based training.

See training as a key tool for executing your company's strategy. Learning objectives are fine, but how do they relate to the company's vision? Are you using training to share knowledge, manage change, and understand the needs of your employees?

During this chapter we will explore how to weave stories into any training event. I will offer ideas on

1. How to select a story
2. How to tell a story
3. How to discuss a story

In the next chapter I will present a few of my favorite story exercises.

HOW TO SELECT A STORY

Stories used in a presentation potentiate a message. If you are giving a speech or presentation, you know ahead of time what you want to communicate. Picking effective stories involves a reflective process. Imagine listening to your presentation for the first time and try to anticipate people's questions. What do you want to emphasize? Where can you use illustrations and examples to strengthen your message? What experiences can you share? This reflective process will begin to trigger story ideas.

Try not to limit yourself. Allow your mind to search freely through its index. Stories come in many shapes and sizes. There are personal stories, anecdotes, scenes and characters from movies, cultural stories, daily observations or interactions, newspaper articles, jokes, metaphors, quotes, and more.

However, if you are not giving the presentation and instead are functioning as a facilitator, you may not know ahead of time everything you are going to say. You will need to listen to the participants carefully and then respond. The "reflective process" of selecting a story is the same as it is when planning a presentation, but it happens more quickly. You will be thinking on your feet. Rely on members of the group to help you. By posing questions and making connections between people's questions and the stories you tell, you will be able to trigger examples and stories from the group. You need not to always have a story. Being able to trigger stories in others is just as important—and oftentimes it is even more effective. The group will be more energized and take ownership if they offer an example.

HOW TO TELL A STORY

There is an art to telling a story. It's important to remember that everyone has a different personality. Your personality will influence your storytelling style. There is no right way to tell a story. I am reminded of what a funny scene a colleague of mine and I must make when we tell stories together. We often tell stories to children in English and Spanish. I'll start to tell the story in English and he translates it into Spanish. I become very excited. I jump around the room flapping my arms up and down. My eyes grow large, and my voice bellows with energy. My colleague on the other hand is calm. He barely moves and he has one of those soft, deep, mellow voices. He is subtler but just as effective if not more so. So what makes us effective?

Whatever your personality, there are three essential aspects to telling a story:

1. A desire to connect
2. Sensitivity to the moods, needs, and desires of a group
3. Reliving the story as you tell it

A Desire to Connect

You have to want to communicate. Whether you are introverted or extroverted doesn't matter. In Part I of the book, we learned how stories create an environment and help people to bind and bond with one another. When you tell a story, focus on your desire to reach out. Sharing a story is a genuine response. It's intimate. Imagine a person who is either sad or depressed. Now imagine a special conversation with a loved one. What's different between the two images? Have you ever noticed how difficult it is for a person who is depressed to communicate? He or she will not want to make eye contact, and you have to work hard to get any response at all, whereas an intimate conversation with a loved one is filled with stories. You have so much you want to share. Think of storytelling—whatever the venue or purpose—as an intimate conversation. When you have something you want to communicate, using a story will have the greatest impact.

Sensitivity to the Moods, Needs, and Desires of the Group

The moods, needs, and desires of a group dictate when to tell a story and what story to tell them. Have you ever told a joke and gotten no response? Or made an excellent comment or point that went unheard because you picked the wrong time to voice it? As a storyteller you must learn how to tune into the dynamics of a group. Stories require active listening. Actively listening to a group is more difficult because there are more people you need to be aware of. Here are some things to look for:

Things to look for	How to use a story
Are people asking similar questions?	Answer their questions with a story.
	Questions are good. It means people are thinking. Get people to draw parallels between the story you tell and the questions they are asking. Provide analysis and insights about the story when people become stuck.
Is there any common theme to the comments people are making?	Elicit stories from the group.
	Try to tie people's comments together. Ask them to be specific and give examples. They will end up sharing personal experiences. Synthesize their comments with their experiences to make new points and to reinforce previous ones.
Do people need an idea or concept to be illustrated?	Use a metaphor or analogy.
	Help people to visualize the idea or concept you are trying to explain by applying a metaphor or analogy from another domain. After you provide one, ask them to think of another one. This solidifies the concept for them and gives them

	confidence. It also allows you to make sure they have grasped the concept.
What is the group's energy?	Tell a story to change the group's energy.
	There are natural ebbs and flows to a group's energy. A story can stimulate and revitalize a group. Likewise, stories can help a group relax and become centered.
What are people saying with their body language?	Tell a story with your voice and body body language?
	When you tell a story, match the tone and body language of individuals in the group. People will become more aware of what they are saying through their bodies and begin to modify their body language. As they do so, there will be subtle shifts in their perceptions and emotions.
Are there underlying emotions?	Validate and transform emotions with a story.
	Tell a story that mirrors the emotions you sense in the group in a non-didactic and unpatronizing way. This validates unspoken emotions and allows people to move past them. Once negative feelings are acknowledged, they can be examined safely through the story and even transformed into more positive ones.
Has the group become stuck?	Tell a story to change their perspective.
	Stories can be used as tools to encourage thinking. A group becomes stuck when it is unable to imagine other possibilities. Stories can be rich sources of irony and paradox. These, in turn, challenge a group's current thinking and can move them in new directions.
Has the group become too analytical?	Use a joke or tangent.
	Jokes are a great tool for getting people to be less analytical. Jokes are like little epiphanies. A joke is funny because the punch line is unexpected. It hits us as a surprise. Telling a joke or leaving the subject at hand to go off on a tangent will help a group become less analytical and more creative.

Reliving the Story as You Retell It

Stories are in danger of becoming static and ineffectual if they are memorized like a script. Remembering a story involves reliving the details as you tell it. Since stories are an oral tradition, many of the details change over time. When I tell a story, I always try to introduce new details that are relevant to the group I am telling it to. Groups respond well to story tailoring. It makes the story special and increases the group's interest, attention, participation, and retention.

I know I am telling a story well when I am surprised by what the characters say and by the events in the story as they unfold. Reliving a story as you tell it makes it easier to keep a large catalogue of indexed stories in your mind. The stories are compressed, but they expand to their full size once you start to tell them. The story seems more real and engaging to the audience, as well as to the teller. For the teller, the story takes on new shades of meaning and enables him or her to discover new insights.

Here are some techniques for telling a story well:

Technique	Description
Voice	Your voice brings a story alive. Think of your voice as an instrument. Instruments are played with dynamics (i.e., sometimes loud, sometimes soft).
	• Animate the stories you tell by varying the pitch, tone, and volume of your voice.
	• Use your voice to guide listeners. Emphasize key words, phrases, or details.
	• Change your voice to represent characters in your story.
	• Insert brief pauses and other rhythmical speech variations.
Repetition	Stories are filled with repetition. These patterns help listeners remember a story and reflect on it later. As a result of repetition, listeners are more actively involved because they are anticipating a recurring theme or pattern.
	• Repeat descriptive details.
	• Select vivid and multisensorial words and reuse them throughout your story.
	• Give listeners a vocal or bodily cue before repeating a pattern.

Participation Stories are more engaging when people participate. When you tell a story, do everything you can to involve your audience. The result? People will listen more carefully and get more out of the story.

- Customize the details of your story to fit the group it is being told to.
- Allow listeners to fill in descriptive, noncritical details of a story.
- In your story, use the names, facts, and characteristics of individuals in the group.
- Include in the story comments individuals have made during the session.
- Weave recent events into your stories.
- Incorporate repetitive elements and have your listeners fill them in.
- Use rhetorical questions.

Body language A story is told with the voice and the body. Have you ever watched a good mime? Body language can communicate more than words.

- Make eye contact with individuals.
- Develop special gestures and postures for story situations and characters.
- Act out parts of the story.
- Use props.
- Move around the room as you tell the story.

It may seem as if this a lot to be aware of when telling a story, but these things happen naturally when you are connected to the story and to the people you are telling it to.

HOW TO DISCUSS A STORY

Stories must always be followed by a brief moment of silence. People need a chance to think about the story before they can respond to it. Even though you may have a very specific reason for telling a story, it is imperative that you resist the urge to tell people the "moral," "meaning," or "purpose" of it. To lead a good discussion, be open to being surprised by the story and its effects on others.

Allow people to react to a story before asking them to be analytical. Start a discussion with a few questions. Probe people's feelings. If a person has a strong reaction to a story, it could provide a source of rich information about him or her. Why is he or she react-ing so strongly? Evidently, the story triggered something in the listener. Be prepared; it may have stirred something totally unre-lated to the apparent thrust of the story. Make an effort to get the person to articulate his or her reaction in terms of another story (e.g., an image, metaphor, or personal experience). The mind works first in stories. It will be easier for someone to respond with a story than to decipher his or her reaction intellectually. Stories have a habit of interconnecting with one another. In a person's mind, one story mingles with another. It is your job as a facilitator to un-tangle the associations and help people generate new ones.

One effect technique is to place people inside a story. You might say to them, "If you had been so and so, what would you have said or done?" This gets them thinking within the story's frame of refer-ence. By entering a story, people leave behind their critical mind and engage their imaginations. Story analysis is an interpretative art; you do not want people rushing to find the "right answer." Dis-cussing a story means reexperiencing it and exploring it from as many angles as possible.

SUMMARY

Stories are central to training and facilitation. People learn bet-ter when they are able to relate new ideas and concepts to their own experiences and base of knowledge. In training, stories are more a way of communicating and dialoguing with people than a specific technique or exercise.

Chapter 7

Exercises to Develop Story Skills That Can Be Used in Training

In this chapter I share with you some of my favorite workshop exercises. These exercises are flexible and can be used to accomplish a variety of objectives. I have used them to teach specific story skills in "story workshops," and I have also used them in more general ways. For the most part they are simple to lead but can have some profound effects on people. Here is a summary of the exercises:

Exercise	Objectives
1. Tell me who you are	Experience storytelling as a more active and effective way of communicating.
	Build rapport between people.
	Enable participants to discover they have a wealth of stories.
	Discover the difference between didactic forms of communication and storytelling.
2. Family story	Practice telling stories.
	Practice listening to stories.
	Learn storytelling techniques.
	Identify what makes one story more interesting than another.
	Encounter the role vulnerability plays in stories.

3. The story of the man who had no stories	Explore how stories work.
	Practice analyzing a story.
	Discover how stories encode information.
4. Story prompts	Illustrate how stories can be triggered.
	Practice looking for connections and relationships between things.
5. Grab bag	Illustrate how stories can be triggered.
	Work with random objects to remember stories.
	Practice looking for connections and relationships between things.
6. Clichés	Find a story to illustrate a cliché.
	Use stories to visualize abstractions.
	Practice thinking in stories.
	Practice telling stories.
7. Capture and recapture	Record a memory and see how others reconstruct it.
	Understand the relationships between memories, perceptions, and stories.
8. Story dialogue	Become aware of how stories are part of communicating.
	Conduct a conversation with only stories.
9. Story cards	Use a deck of cards to construct a story in order to gain insights into a question or issue.
	Discover how to craft stories to interpret things.
10. Joanna Macy's learning to see each other	Learn to shift your perspective to compassionately encounter another person.
	Demonstrate the role of empathy in stories.
	Imagine another person's perspective.

EXERCISE 1: TELL ME WHO YOU ARE

Duration: 50–60 minutes

Instructions

1. Have people pair off, if possible with someone they do not know.
2. Instruct one person to talk about himself or herself while the other sits and listens. The listener cannot ask any questions or say anything.

3. After 10 to 15 minutes, have them switch roles.

4. Debrief the exercise.

Facilitating

This is an interesting exercise to watch. For one thing, many people dislike talking about themselves. They feel that they have very little to say, and that their lives are not very interesting. Typically, people approach the exercise like an interview. They begin rattling off the facts of their lives (e.g., where they were born, raised, went to school, and worked). Before long they run out of things to say, but there is usually a lot of time left. Without realizing what they are doing, they begin telling a story. Suddenly time begins to compress, they realize they have a lot to say, and they become more animated. You can also observe a change in the listeners. Listeners lean forward and become more involved in what the person is saying.

After the exercise, get people to share their experiences and observations. See whether they can identify when they switched into a storytelling mode versus a fact-relating mode. Go around the room and have people give examples. Encourage them to draw parallels between the exercise and communication in general. See whether people can recall similar experiences, such as when they had trouble communicating or used a story.

EXERCISE 2: FAMILY STORY

Duration: 90–120 minutes

Instructions

1. Create groups of four or five people.

2. Have everyone in the group tell two or more family or childhood stories. The stories should be about the participant or about a relative, sibling, or childhood friend.

3. The group listens to each story, selects two to tell to the group at large, and designates a spokesperson.

4. Have each group tell the stories it selected.

5. Debrief the exercises.

Variation

This exercise also works well with pairs. Have each person select one of the partner's stories and retell it to the group.

Facilitating

This exercise gives people experience in active listening. Retelling another person's story and bringing it alive for others is not as easy as it may seem. In order to experience a story, the imagination must be actively working. Have people pay attention to how much detail they include. Ask those recounting the stories to explain why they selected them.

Ask the person whom the story is about to evaluate the telling of it. Use your judgment. If you think it is appropriate, ask the originator to suggest any insights the story provides about him or her as a person. Don't be surprised; this often happens without your even asking. Throw the same question out to the group at large. This is especially fascinating when people know each other fairly well. Be careful, because you may get more than you bargained for. Stories are very revealing. A story can provide a powerful looking glass into a person. However, it can also be used to reinforce inaccurate and self-serving perceptions. So you will have to handle these discussions with care.

EXERCISE 3: THE STORY OF THE MAN WHO HAD NO STORIES

Duration: 90 minutes

Instructions

1. Tell the following story to the group.
2. After telling the story, create groups of four or five.
3. Hand out a copy of the story.
4. Instruct people to read the story on their own and then discuss it with their group.
5. Give each group a flip chart. Ask the groups to analyze the story. What can they learn from it about the nature of stories?
6. Let the groups work for thirty minutes.
7. Start a group discussion by asking each group to report on its work.

Here is the story:

> Liam was a basket weaver. He would cut rushes, make them into baskets, and sell them in the nearby towns. After some time, there were no rushes left.
>
> He knew of a glen far away where fine rushes were reputed to grow. But it was a fairy glen and nobody dared go

there. However, Liam's money had run out, and he was desperate, so he decided to take a risk. With his knife, a rope, and the lunch his wife packed for him, Liam set out for the glen.

He had cut two fine bundles and tied them together when a thick mist began to form around him. Thinking the fog would clear soon, he decided to sit down and eat his lunch. By the time he had finished eating, he could not even see his hands.

Liam became disoriented. He stood up and looked to the east and looked to the west. Off in the distance he saw a light and he thought, "Where there is light there's bound to be people." So he set out for the light and eventually came upon a farmhouse with the door standing open. Liam entered and found an old man and woman sitting by a fire. "Come in and get warm," they said. And then after exchanging some pleasantries, the old man asked him to tell a story.

"I can't," said Liam. "I've never told a story."

The woman turned to him and said, "Then go down to the well and bring us a bucket of water for your keep."

"I'd be happy to, as long as I don't have to tell a story," replied Liam.

Liam went down to the well and filled the bucket. He set the bucket down for a moment so that the outside of it could dry before he brought it in. Suddenly, the wind roared and swept him high into the sky. It blew him to the east, and it blew him to the west. When he fell back to Earth, there was no bucket, and no well, and no farmhouse. But again, off in the distance, he saw a light and he thought, "Where there is light there's bound to be people." So he set out for the light, and after some time, he found that it came from a farmhouse far bigger than the first, with lights shining out of the door.

When he entered, Liam saw that he had come to a wakehouse. There were two rows of men sitting by the back wall, and a girl with black curly hair sat by the fire. She welcomed Liam and asked him to sit beside her.

Liam had barely sat down when a big man stood up. "It's not a real wake without a fiddler. I'll go get one so that we can start dancing."

"Don't go," said the girl with black curly hair. "The best fiddler in Ireland is here." And she looked straight at Liam.

"Oh, no," said Liam. "I can't play a tune on a fiddle. I've got no music in my head."

"Sure you can," insisted the girl with black curly hair, and she pushed a fiddle and bow into his hand and he played away. And everyone agreed they had never heard a better fiddler than Liam.

They danced and danced until the big man said that was enough. "We must go get a priest to say Mass. This corpse must leave before daybreak."

"There's no need," said the girl with black curly hair. "The best priest in Ireland is sitting right here." And again she looked straight at Liam.

"Oh no," said Liam. "I'm no priest. I know nothing about a priest's work."

"Sure you do," she said. "You will do it just as well as you did the fiddling."

So before Liam knew it, he was standing at the altar saying Mass. And they all said that they'd never heard any priest say a better Mass than Liam.

Then the corpse was put in the coffin, and four men took it on their shoulders. Three were short and one was tall, and the coffin wobbled terribly.

"We'll have to go get a doctor to cut a piece off the leg of that big man to make him the same length as the others," said one of the men.

"Stay here," said the girl with black curly hair. "The best doctor in all of Ireland is here among us." And again she looked straight at Liam.

"Oh no," said Liam. "I've never done any doctoring. I couldn't possibly do it."

"Sure you can," she said.

And she thrust a scalpel into his hand. Liam cut a piece out of each of the big man's legs, under his knees, and stuck the legs back on and made him the same height as the other three. Everyone marveled at Liam's doctoring skills and all agreed they had never seen a better doctor in all of Ireland.

They picked up the coffin and walked carefully to the graveyard. There was a big stone wall around the graveyard, ten feet high or maybe twelve. They all climbed the wall to the graveyard on the other side. The last man on top of the wall was Liam.

But a big blast of wind swept him into the sky. It blew him to the east and it blew him to the west. When he fell back to Earth there was no graveyard, or wall, or coffin, or funeral. He had fallen by the well where he had gone to fetch some water. The water had not even dried off the bucket.

Liam took the bucket into the house. The old man and woman were there just as he had left them. He put the bucket down beside them.

"Now, Liam," said the old man, "can you tell us a story?"

"I can," said he. "I am a man with a story to tell." And he told them about everything that had happened to him.

"Well, Liam," said the old man, "from now on, if anybody asks you to tell a story, tell them that story; you are a man who has a story to tell."

They gave him a bed, and Liam fell asleep, for he was tired after all he had gone through.

And when he woke in the morning, he was lying in the fairy glen with his head on the two bundles of rushes. He got up and went home and he never worked another day in his life.

Facilitating

Practice telling the story. It is important that you are comfortable with the story. I also suggest rereading the first section of the book to review the different ways stories can function. Use the charts at the end of each chapter or Appendix B as a guide.

This story always generates lots of rich discussion. If people get stuck, have them step back and offer some ideas on what a story is, and how and why a story works. Then turn their attention back to the text.

EXERCISE 4: STORY PROMPTS

Duration: 60–90 minutes

Instructions

1. Draw two columns on a flip chart or board and label them "roles" and "actions."

Roles	Actions

2. Instruct people to think about all of the various roles they play at work and at home and write them down.

3. Now create a list of things they do (actions). Help them out by suggesting that one way of generating a list is to think about what actions they perform in the roles they listed.

4. Give them some examples and then let them work on their own for twenty minutes or so.

5. Take a role from the left side and try to match it up randomly with an action on the right side. Do one or two examples to demonstrate how to use the list of roles and actions to trigger stories. Give them five minutes to look at their list and trigger stories.

6. Go around the room and ask people to share a story or two and indicate what sets of roles and actions they used to trigger the story.

Facilitating

Be sure to provide plenty of examples. I try to avoid examples I have used with other groups. I want my stories and the triggers that aroused them to be fresh and spontaneous each time I facilitate this exercise. Participants need to see triggers in actions. That's what has the greatest impact.

As you begin paying more attention to stories, triggering them becomes easier. Each of us has some sort of schema in our mind that indexes stories. This exercise lets people experience how to access and stimulate their indexes. Participants discover how to see interrelationships between ostensibly disconnected roles and actions.

Be supportive of people who find this exercise difficult. If necessary, randomly select an action and role for them. You may have others who are very clever. Push them to dig deeper.

EXERCISE 5: GRAB BAG

Duration: 3–5 minutes per person

Instructions

1. Fill a bag with random objects.
2. Have each person draw an object.
3. Go around the room and have people use the object to trigger a story.
4. Be sure to include yourself in the exercise.

Facilitation

I love a story my father-in-law told me. Sam works as a funeral director. He and his colleagues routinely challenged a certain rabbi. Before a funeral service they would give the rabbi a word—for example, "ice cream." The rabbi had to find a way of incorporating this word into his eulogy. Without fail and to the utter amazement of Sam and his colleagues, no matter what the word was, the rabbi managed to find a connection between the word and the person he was speaking about.

This exercise is like the anecdote about the rabbi. Participants are challenged to take an object and generate a story. This can be a nice way to wrap up a day's activities, or to reenergize a group after a difficult or draining exercise.

Try to get people to think beyond the creative aspects of cleverly fashioning a story from a random object. You want them to extend the idea of interconnectedness beyond random objects and stories. They should see that one experience or story is an opportunity to trigger another one and gain new insights. As discussed in the introductory chapter and advanced by Roger Schank, one of the hallmarks of intelligence is the capacity to apply stories from one domain to another.

EXERCISE 6: CLICHÉS

Duration: 3–5 minutes per person

Instructions

1. Write out some of your favorite clichés or aphorisms on index cards.

Here are a few to get you started:

"Don't cut off your nose to spite your face."

"If life gives you lemons, make lemonade."

"If at first you don't succeed, try, try, again."

"At the drop of a hat."

"You can't judge a book by its cover."

"A stitch in time saves nine."

"Live for today."

"You can't see the forest for the trees."

"It's water under the bridge."

"What you see is what you get."

"What's here today is gone tomorrow."

2. Have each participant pick an index card at random.

3. Go around the room and have people tell a story triggered by the cliché they picked.

Facilitation

This exercise gives participants confidence in triggering, indexing, and crafting stories quickly. Clichés are abstract in nature and are criticized as overused phrases that lack specificity. Participants will see how stories bring abstractions to life. How does the story they tell connect to the cliché? Instead of articulating an idea abstractly, how quickly can they find an appropriate story to express their ideas? Help the group imagine how replacing an abstraction with a story will enable them to communicate more clearly.

EXERCISE 7: CAPTURE AND RECAPTURE

Duration: 60 minutes

Instructions

1. At the end of the day, instruct everyone to take an index card and write down either something that happened or something that was said during the session that really sticks out in his or her mind.

2. On the following day, have each participant randomly draw an index card.

3. Ask the participant to recount the event or the things that were said that led up to the event or to comment on the index card.

4. Compare the participant's recounting and interpretation of the event's significance with that of the person who wrote the card and with the perceptions of the rest of the group.

Facilitation

This is not an easy exercise to facilitate. You may have to run this a few times before you get the hang of it. The problem is, not every index card will yield a vigorous discussion. One suggestion I have is to read all of the cards first and select the more interesting or potentially provocative ones.

If a particular index card is not generating discussion, quickly move on to another one. Be sure to choose carefully the person who goes first. It should be someone who you are confident can reconstruct the previous day's event or comment. However, there's no need to worry. If that person is unable to tell a story, that is an important insight in and of itself. What sticks out in one person's mind as memorable may not be important or have even registered in the memory of another.

After one person attempts to give his or her account, ask the author of the index card to share his or her recollection. How do the two accounts differ? Next, ask the group at large to share its memories and perceptions. Are there more differences?

This exercise demonstrates the role of perception. Try to help participants discover how stories are a powerful way of understanding our perceptions and those of others.

EXERCISE 8: STORY DIALOGUE

Duration: 60 minutes

Instructions

1. Have people pair off.
2. Give each pair a list of conversational topics. Create a list of topics for participants to choose from. Here are a few ideas:

- School and teachers
- Holidays
- Summer vacations
- Travel
- Food
- Children

3. The topics can be about anything. Your list of topics can be generic like those mentioned, or it can be more specific to the people and situation. In some circumstances, I ask the pairs to come up with their own topics.

4. One person in the pair begins a conversation by telling a story. Each partner must respond to a story with a story.

5. Each person should make a record of the conversation. This only needs to be a word or two to jar each other's memory as to the conversation's development and progression.

6. Give people fifteen minutes for their story conversations.

7. Go around the room and have people describe their conversations in turn.

Facilitation

This exercise helps people to see the role stories can play in conversation. The best response to a story is another story. However, be sure to emphasize that storytelling is not about outdoing each other with wilder and wilder tales. Rather, stories generate opportunities for defining common ground and understanding each other's experiences.

Ask the pairs to share the twists and turns of their conversation. They should use their notes to help them. Get participants to reflect on how their partner's stories triggered stories. Inquire how all of the stories interrelate.

Ask them to characterize the overall effect of stories. See whether they perceive any difference between an average conversation and one from a story. Can they imagine using stories in their daily conversations? See if someone can offer an example of a recent conversation. How would that conversation have been different if stories had been used?

EXERCISE 9: STORY CARDS

Duration: 10–30 minutes per card reading

Instructions

There are a lot of variations to this exercise. I will offer a few, but I encourage you to experiment.

Jean Adi, a gifted artist friend of mine, designed a deck of cards that I use in workshops and with clients. (For information on ordering your own deck, see Appendix D.) The color and graphics on the card help people generate images and stories.

If you do not have a deck, take fifty-two index cards and write the following phrases on them:

1. Best way to learn

2. Empowered
3. Environment
4. Bind and bond
5. Harken
6. Negotiate
7. Encoded
8. Argument
9. Stage fright
10. Healing
11. Thinking tool
12. Tools of the trade
13. Let me entertain you
14. Bridging the gap
15. The critical point in the system
16. Uncover
17. Hidden agenda
18. Frame of reference
19. Boxed in
20. Making connections
21. The weaver
22. Soar like an eagle
23. Alternative role
24. Casting error
25. Exception to the rule
26. Defy definition
27. Smart thinking
28. Rule of thumb
29. Acts of revolt
30. Be kind
31. Breathe
32. Stagnation
33. Time and money
34. Truth and courage
35. Pocket of ignorance
36. Quantum leap
37. The dark night
38. The art of . . .
39. Mutual exchange

40. Verge of success
41. Shouting for joy
42. The verdict
43. Heart of practice
44. Resolve a conflict
45. Looking back
46. Peaks and valleys
47. Cause and effect
48. Change in pressure
49. Brain sucker
50. Snap, crackle, and pop
51. Take a bow
52. Stay here

Instruct the person receiving the reading to shuffle the deck and think of a work-related question. Have him or her cut the deck of cards and tell you the question. Holding the deck, have the subject select five cards. Put the cards in a row face down and have the subject turn them over one at a time. Tell a story with the cards. Finish a card reading by asking the person to offer comments.

Variations

1. Try varying the number of cards.
2. Let the person asking the question give the reading.
3. Do a sample reading with a group, and then have people pair off and do readings for each other.
4. Draw a single card and use it as a "story trigger."
5. Develop a list of phrases and words that fit your company or situation.
6. I know some managers who use their deck of cards during meetings to generate discussion and gain insight into people's thoughts and feelings.

Facilitation

This exercise is fun to facilitate because people really get into the reading. I believe it's the fortune-teller-like character of it that fascinates people. I am reminded of an anecdote you have probably heard before, about people lost on a mountain. One person has a map. The party uses the map to find its way home, only to realize at the end that the map was not of the mountain. These story cards are meant to be like that map. The cards are effective because they trigger stories and images. Faced with a pattern and a concrete representation, we can generate meaning and discover insights we habitually thrust below the surface in the name of rationality. The cards encourage us to see possibilities and relationships.

You can be as light or as serious as you like. Be careful to avoid pushing your own agenda. When you know a lot about a person or situation, you are likely to be able to find a way to use the cards to communicate and validate your perspective. Try to avoid doing this. Make every effort to be as open and impartial as you can be. Until you get the hang of it, let people do their own readings. When they are finished, you can offer a few ideas of your own.

EXERCISE 10: JOANNA MACY'S LEARNING TO SEE EACH OTHER

(Reprinted from *World As Lover, World As Self* [1991] by Joanna Macy with permission of Parallax Press, Berkeley, California.)

Duration: 45 minutes

Instructions

1. Have people pair off and face one another.
2. Explain the exercise. You will be reading a meditation written by Joanna Macy. During the meditation, each person will sit across from his or her partner and stare into the other's eyes. At times it may be uncomfortable! We are not accustomed to looking into each other's eyes. Encourage people to relax and focus on the words of the meditation being read.
3. Read the meditation in a slow and gentle voice.
4. Discuss the meditation.

Meditation

Take a couple of deep breaths, centering yourself and exhaling tension. . . . Look into each other's eyes. . . . If you feel discomfort or an urge to laugh or look away, just note that embarrassment with patience and gentleness, and come back, when you can, to your partner's eyes. You may never see this person again: the opportunity to behold the uniqueness of this particular human being is given to you now. . . .

As you look into this person's eyes, let yourself become aware of the powers that are there.... Open your awareness to the gifts and strengths and potentialities in this being. . . . Behind those eyes are unmeasured reserves of courage and intelligence . . . of patience, endurance, wit and wisdom. . . . There are gifts there, of which this person her/himself is unaware. . . . Consider what these powers could do for the healing of our planet, if they were believed and acted on. . . . As you consider that, let yourself become aware of your desire that this person be free from fear, free from greed, released from hatred and from sorrow and from the causes of suffering. . . . Know that what you are now experiencing is the great loving-kindness. . . .

Now as you look into those eyes, let yourself become aware of the pain that is there. There are sorrows accumulated in that life, as in all human lives, though you can only guess at them. There are disappointments and failures and losses and loneliness and abuse . . . there are hurts beyond the telling. . . . Let yourself open to that pain, to hurts that this person may never have told another being. . . . You cannot fix that pain but you can be with it. As you let yourself simply be with that suffering, know what you are experiencing is the great compassion. It is very good for the healing of our world.

As you look into the eyes of this person, consider how good it would be to work together . . . on a joint project, toward a common goal. . . . What it could be like, taking risks together . . . conspiring together in zest and laughter . . . celebrating the successes, consoling each other over the setbacks, forgiving each other when you make mistakes . . . and simply being there for each other. . . . As you open to that possibility, what you open to is the great wealth: the pleasure in each other's power, the joy in each other's joy.

Lastly, let your awareness drop deep within you like a stone, sinking below the level of what words can express, to the deep web of relationship that underlies all experience. It is the web of life in which you have taken being, in which you are supported, and that interweaves us through all space and time. . . . See the being before you as if seeing the face of one who, at another time, another place, was your lover or your enemy, your parent or your child. . . . And now you meet again on this brink of time. . . . And you know your lives are as intricately interwoven as nerve cells in the mind of a great being. . . . Out of that vast net you cannot fall . . . no stupidity, or failure, or cowardice, can ever sever you from that living web. For that is what you are. : . . Rest in that knowing. Rest in the Great Peace. . . . Out of it we can act, we can venture everything . . . and let every encounter be a homecoming to our true nature. . . . Indeed it is so.

Facilitation

Once when I used this exercise, two people who had never met one another before paired off. At the end of the meditation, the woman turned to the man and inquired, "Did your father die recently?"

The man was shocked. His father had died two weeks earlier. He asked her, "How could you possibly know?"

She replied, "I saw it in your eyes."

This is a powerful exercise. The ability to see things from another person's perspective is a fundamental but largely dormant human capacity. During your discussion with the group, help them sort through their feelings and reactions. (Note that you should not do this exercise if you have not been through it yourself.) One of the first times I did this exercise as a participant, I became so self-conscious at times that I began to smirk and giggle. Be prepared. Some people may see no value in the exercise or even become angry.

You will need to help the group understand the business imperatives and broad implications of compassion. Ask them what role compassion plays in business. Why is it an important quality for a leader or manager? Putting aside the humanitarian aspects, compassion enables us to tune in to the needs and concerns of the people we work with, and the customers we serve. Stories are a way of standing in another person's shoes, and of sharing our shoes with others.

SUMMARY

The exercises in this chapter are a few of the ones I use when giving a workshop on stories or management and leadership topics, but they are by no means an exhaustive list. Whether you are involved in instructional design or giving a workshop with a completely technical focus, stories are the most effective means for transmitting and receiving information.

Chapter 8

======

The Role of Stories in Business Processes and Knowledge Management

Among other things, in the future companies will be competitively affected by

1. How they attract, develop, and train people
2. How they capture, manage, and share knowledge across the enterprise
3. How they organizationally structure the company

Earlier we touched on the relationship between stories and knowledge. Stories are efficient encoders of information. Every story or experience is a wealth of knowledge waiting to be tapped. To be effective, stories must be exchanged and assimilated. How do we create an environment that stimulates storytelling? Within companies, stories will have to function like a network of neurons firing constantly so that employees can communicate with one another and create new connections.

This chapter examines the role stories can play in understanding business processes and knowledge management. The next chapter looks at the relationship between stories and the organizational development challenge of managing corporate culture, leadership, and change.

USING STORIES TO UNDERSTAND
BUSINESS PROCESSES

The word "competency" is grossly overused. How can we be so focused on competency and yet have so much incompetency and job dissatisfaction in the workplace? People do not fit into cast roles, and most jobs cannot be defined by a simple description of the requisite abilities.

Looking for competency can trick us into "black and white thinking." Individuals are labeled and evaluated based on whether they possess a skill. For example: Departmental manager needs to have solid project management skills.

I doubt if you could get a roomful of people to agree on a definition of "solid project management skills." Even if we reach consensus, we still have to determine whether someone meets that definition. It is hardly a "yes" or "no" proposition. It is more useful to speak in terms of degrees, where "yes" is equal to some ideal state of project management skills, and "no" is equal to a state of no such skills. Surely, those individuals we recruit, interview, hire, and train will fit somewhere along this continuum.

Competency modeling presents other challenges. Companies spend a lot of time examining job descriptions and defining competencies, but few companies regularly revisit them. Part of the problem is that companies consist of functional areas. Each area has a number of jobs, and for every job there is a set number of tasks and responsibilities. Competencies are determined by understanding these tasks and responsibilities:

Job Title	Tasks, Responsibilities	Competencies
Payroll specialist	Collect time sheets	Attention to detail
	Enter time sheets	Time management skills
	Print reports	Analytical skills
	Research problems	Problem-solving skills
	Resolve discrepancies	Communication skills
	Submit payroll	Computer skills

Competitive pressures and information technology are forcing us to rethink how we organize and manage companies. Companies are beginning to look more like self-organizing systems. A single employee may spend one day a week as a payroll specialist, another day as a buyer, and another as a financial analyst. The number of jobs that can be easily defined in terms of consistent tasks and responsibilities is rapidly shrinking. We cannot rely on being able to control organizations by breaking them into simple functional areas. Information must move quickly across many areas of an organization. Therefore, it has become far more important to understand business processes.

We will define business processes in a straightforward way. They have two characteristics. First, they have defined business outcomes that have either internal or external customers. And second, they normally occur across or between functional areas or subunits of the organization.

Let's examine how to elicit, collect, and analyze stories to capture business processes. The stories collected will shed light on how things get done, how the most effective employees get things done, how to make current processes more effective, what new processes or best practices the organization should adopt, and what talents the organization needs. An array of competencies and talents can be garnered from these stories. Keep in mind that this array will evolve along with the business as its processes change and adapt.

Eliciting and Collecting Stories

The "institutional memory" of an organization rests in its people and their stories. It's important to examine an organization's history in order to understand why things are currently done the way they are. Seek out individuals who have had a long tenure with the organization. You will quickly gain their respect and trust if you show a genuine interest in their stories and perspectives. Simple questions can elicit stories:

1. What was the company like twenty years ago?
2. If you had been president and CEO, what things would you have done differently?
3. What was your first job?
4. How has your job changed over the years?
5. What aspect of your work are you most proud of?
6. In your opinion, who were the most effective leaders?
7. How has the company's image changed?
8. What makes this company unique?
9. What are the strengths of the company?
10. What are its weaknesses?

Be sure to ask follow-up questions. Look for stories, not just descriptions. If a particular question does not yield a story, try rephrasing it. Stories are indexed mentally and everyone indexes them in different ways. Some words will not trigger a person's index. Therefore, you will have to pay careful attention to the language people use and to the questions and language to which they respond well.

By the time you finish collecting stories about the company's history, you will have formed some theories about the evolution of the company, its product and services, and the jobs that are involved. Your next task is to develop a map detailing

1. Who the company's customers (both external and internal) are
2. What products or services they receive
3. What functional areas of the company are involved in delivering the products or services
4. Within each functional area, what job titles are involved in delivering the products or services
5. What tasks are performed by the employees with these job titles

See Figure 8.1 for a chart to get you started.

Using your map as a guide, interview employees. Seek employees who are effective at their jobs and who have a unique way of handling their tasks and responsibilities. It is not as useful to talk to people who do things "by the book"; you do not need to talk to people to understand normal procedures and policies. However, unless you can capture stories, you will never learn how the better employees work within and around the policies and procedures, and how these can be improved as the company moves forward.

You will need to use two techniques. First, whenever possible, shadow an employee for a while to see him or her in action. Observe what personal characteristics and work relationships make the employee effective. Second, ask questions to elicit stories:

1. How did you learn to do your job?
2. Who taught you how to do your job?
3. How did the person who taught you do the job?
4. Can you give me examples of how your tasks and responsibilities have changed?
5. What makes you so effective?
6. What experiences have shaped the way you do your job?
7. Over the years, have you developed any new skills?
8. What prompted you to develop those skills?
9. Use a recent example to explain how you would streamline your current tasks and responsibilities.
10. How would you coach a new employee to do your job?

Figure 8.1
Map to Detail Customers Products and Services

Customer	Products and Services	Functional Areas	Job Titles	Tasks
External				
Internal				

Next, take all of the stories you have collected and begin to draw your own conclusions. Your results will likely fall into one of the following categories.

Simplification and Process Improvement

These are business processes that over time have grown too complicated. For example, there might be too many steps in a process. Through your interviews you discover that there are easier ways to get the same things done. The more successful employees have found ways of shaving time off the process or leveraging their informal relationships in the organization to complete the process in a more effective manner.

Automation

The strategic application of technology can improve a business process. Frequently, steps of a process can be either eliminated or sped up with some automation. Business processes that could possibly benefit from automation must be analyzed in terms of return on investment and the impact automation will have on an organization's culture and structure.

Recruiting and Training

As you look at a business process, certain skills and talents may stand out as being critical success factors. In other words, the most effective employees exhibit behavior and characteristics that you want to find in new employees or instill in your existing ones. Training can be designed to develop employees and address performance issues.

Restructuring

In order to improve or automate a business process, it may be necessary to restructure an organization. For example, reducing the number of signatures required to make purchases entails giving employees more autonomy and authority. To do so will require some reorganization.

Business Opportunity

To be competitive, organizations must continually recreate themselves. The stories you collect may provide insights into new products or services that would benefit internal and external customers. Rethinking a business process is an opportunity to invigorate an organization with fresh energy and new ideas.

The stories you collect and analyze may also indicate that a particular business process needs to be left alone. There may be political or historical reasons why things are the way they are; not every process has to be challenged in the ways described. The nuances to be found by examining stories will help you set some priorities. You cannot address all of them at once. List your priorities and develop a strategy for each one. Concentrate on business processes you can improve. Others you may want to defer to a later date, or you may want to find another champion within the organization to carry the idea forward.

KNOWLEDGE MANAGEMENT

Knowledge management is an elusive term. But however one defines it, it is a critical measure of an organization's future competitiveness. Today, companies are scrambling to implement data warehouses, customer relationship management software, enterprise relationship management, and collaboration or groupware systems. These all point to an ongoing effort to capture, store, index, search, and analyze information in order to keep an organization mobile and agile. Access to information allows managers to make better decisions and adjust an organization's strategy on the fly. However, access to information is not enough. One must know when to ask a question, what question to ask, and how to find the answer. Without these, information is of little value.

We know that it no longer makes sense to develop a detailed five-year plan. Such a plan will inevitably end up gathering dust on a shelf. I am not suggesting we abandon strategic planning; I am drawing attention to the fact that as markets change quickly, organizations must learn how to adapt and reinvent themselves just as quickly. Imagine a good boxer. A boxer is never certain of what punch his opponent will throw next, so he stays light on his feet and weaves and bobs his head to keep his opponent off balance. Organizations need to learn how to weave and bob. New ventures will be determined through a series of tests and trials. The perfect product, service, marketing, or pricing model will not be drawn up in the abstract and then implemented. Instead, these things will arise as a series of rapid, ongoing "entrepreneurial" research and development efforts.

To use another metaphor, organizations must become like a well-trained muscle. Muscles have two important attributes: strength and flexibility. If a muscle is too strong, it is incapable of bending. Alternatively, if a muscle is too flexible, it does not have enough strength to support itself. Organizations are challenged to find the perfect balance between strength and flexibility. Plans and strategies are like the strength of a muscle. Generating a strategic plan engenders a "firm" sense of structure and certainty. On the other hand, organizations must remain flexible and open to the feedback they receive. Feedback mechanisms must be used to adjust a strategic plan and rework it as the organization moves toward a common goal.

So how will an organization capture and retain all of the lessons learned in the process of conducting its test and trials? Attempting to keep information in central repositories such as databases and similar sorts of information technology tools will not suffice. These tools imply that the data being stored in them are structured. I use the term "structured data" to describe data that can be easily and neatly classified. However, much of the knowledge in an organization is in the form of unstructured data. People's stories and experiences are an example of unstructured data.

From what we have learned about indexing, we know that stories cannot be mapped to any one indexing scheme. Stories are too rich and contain too much information. The standard tools used today for knowledge management do not handle unstructured data very well. And the ones that try to do so, or will try to do so in the foreseeable future, will not be dynamic or flexible enough.

For example, verbal information moves at blistering speeds. Remember playing the game "telephone"? A group of people form a large circle. One person begins the game by whispering a message to the next person. The message is passed around the circle. By the time the last person in the circle whispers the message to the person who started it, the original message has become completely garbled. Despite the claims of technologists, effective knowledge management will depend more on informal processes established in an organization to promote story swapping than on any system or software.

Every organization will have to experiment in order to find processes that facilitate knowledge transfer. Here are some ideas to get you started:

- Designate special areas and times for story swapping.
- Implement design and project methodologies that incorporate story gathering and telling.
- Include storytelling as an agenda item for key meetings.
- Substantiate strategic and tactical plans with stories and cases.
- Conduct story skill workshops as part of everyone's training.
- Create incentives for people to share their stories.
- Use information technology to exchange stories.
- Treat knowledge as an asset, design ways to measure the increase of it, and reward contributors.

Power is an implicit part of knowledge. The person with knowledge has power. This is why people hesitate to share knowledge. Whether you realize it or not, most organizations promote and reward people who can wield power and use it to benefit the organization's bottom line. Therefore, there is no incentive for anyone to share knowledge. Whatever processes you adopt or try, it is essential that you keep this in mind. People have to be shown that their knowledge is valued in the organization and that they will be rewarded for sharing it. Perhaps we need to reframe our notion of knowledge management. We are not really after the "management" of knowledge, because that's not realistic. Knowledge transforms and transmutes itself too quickly. It is not something that can be nailed down. What is knowledge today is hindsight or even irrelevant tomorrow. The word "management" implies control. We have no control over the lessons learned or the organizational epiphanies that occur along a path of development. We can, however, maximize our inherent story capacity and leverage it in organizations by creating opportunities for others to share their stories.

SUMMARY

In this chapter we have moved away from viewing stories as a singular communication device. We have taken an integrative look at how the power of stories can be used to tackle business processes and knowledge management. Next, we want to see how stories can be used to get our hands around corporate culture, organizational development, and change management. Whatever management trend or theory we subscribe to, stories will play a pivotal role.

Chapter 9

======

The Role of Stories in Corporate Culture, Change Management, and Leadership

Three key areas have a major effect on an organization's growth and health:

1. Corporate culture
2. Change management
3. Leadership

These primary areas involve complex phenomena that are subjects of lengthy discussions. However, with "story thinking," we can simplify how we approach them. I am not offering the three simple steps that are guaranteed to create a thriving corporate culture, a magical formula on how to manage change, or yet another compelling model of leadership. Despite all the books and the bold claims made, there are no easy answers.

This chapter synthesizes everything we have discussed. We are going to use what we have learned about stories to identify strategies for using them to build or modify corporate culture, help employees manage rapid change, and communicate more effectively as leaders.

Here's what we have done so far:

- Broadened our notion of what stories are and left behind any preconceived ideas about what constitutes a story
- Identified how stories function

- Took a quick overview of how stories can be applied to some areas of human resources
- Provided guidelines for how to select a story, how to tell a story, and how to discuss a story
- Assembled a toolbox of exercises that can be used to teach story skills
- Applied storytelling, story listening, and story thinking skills to identify business processes and manage the dissemination and sharing of knowledge

As we become more aware that stories are the way our mind works, it is increasingly easier to understand how they can be applied to complex aspects of business such as corporate culture, change management, and leadership.

CORPORATE CULTURE

Have you noticed how every organization has a unique character? Like people, organizations have personalities. As soon as you enter an organization, you notice things that reflect its culture. Perhaps it's the way the office is decorated or just the way people greet you. Upon careful examination, you can usually point to specific people, historical events, or past and current company policies that influence an organization's culture, but what about some of the more subtle things that are not as obvious?

Corporate culture comprises values and beliefs. The physical things we observe are either an external manifestation of values or, sometimes, obvious flags of incongruence between the real values and desired ones. For example, you may see a poster espousing the values of friendly customer service, yet as you walk around the organization you hear employees interacting with customers and with each other in a cross or impatient manner. By itself, hanging positive posters will not create an atmosphere of friendliness. So where do these values and beliefs come from, and how are they communicated? Stories provide us with profound insights into these matters.

In order to understand all the elements comprising an organization's culture, conduct an audit of the following four key areas:

1. *The Physical Environment.* This consists of all of the things that you can observe about the surroundings. Use the following questions to guide you:
   - How would you characterize the environment?
   - How is it decorated?
   - How does the environment make you feel?

- What is the layout of the office?
- Do people appear comfortable and happy?
- As you enter the reception area, what is your first impression? What things catch your eye?

2. *Written Materials.* A careful examination of internal and external documents will give you a taste of the organization's culture. These include such documents as

   - Mission statement
   - Vision statement
   - Marketing materials
   - Want ads
   - Job descriptions
   - Performance appraisal forms
   - Strategic plans
   - Annual reports
   - Press releases
   - Web sites

3. *Policies and Practices.* Policies and how they are followed or ignored reflect a company's attitude toward its employees. As you read them, keep the following questions in mind:

   - How are the policies worded?
   - What benefits are offered to employees?
   - How much flexibility is there?
   - What are people's attitudes toward the policies?
   - How old are the policies?
   - How easy is it to modify or revise a policy?

4. *Stories.* Stories are your best gauge of an organization's culture. Stories highlight differences between an organization's actual culture, cultural changes it has gone through, and its desired culture. Some stories to look for include

   - How the company got started
   - Stories about the founder(s)
   - New and old stories of customer experiences
   - Stories from veteran employees

An organization's culture affects people's perceptions of the organization both internally and externally. We form many of our opinions and perceptions about organizations and people based on the stories we acquire about them. In other words, stories are defining because they reflect our self-perceptions. Stories also reflect how we want to be perceived. In fact, we usually tell stories that show us in a positive light. It's not uncommon to see employees trying to outdo each other as they swap stories over lunch.

You can tell more about an organization or person from a single story than from long conversations or piles of written materials. The stories that stick out in our minds, and the ones we feel impelled to tell first, encapsulate a lot of information. Think back to the story of Janice Shaker in Chapter 4 during our discussion of how stories encode information. Janice's "quality control" luncheon will stick out in the minds of her employees for a long time. It's a story employees will tell over and over again.

Communication through stories is more succinct and more precise because we enact instead of announce our intentions, thoughts, values, or knowledge. Stories model what we want to communicate instead of explaining it. And as the cliché goes, "Actions speak louder than words."

Using Stories to Modify a Culture

Stories can be used as a tool for modifying a culture. In the example below, a story is used to change the image of a restaurant.

Case Study: The Story of Lilly's on the Pond

Sue Anne had been working in New Hampshire inns and restaurants for over twenty years. It was her dream to buy and manage her own restaurant one day. Her dream came true when she received an unexpected windfall. Sue Anne immediately began shopping for a restaurant to buy, and asked her long time colleagues Helen and Lee to join her.

The Old Forge restaurant in Rindge, New Hampshire, had been around for over a quarter of a century but was going out of business. The beautiful wooden structure situated next to a pond had fallen into complete disrepair. The once famous and cheery place had succumbed to a dark and dreary decor complete with rusty blacksmith tools and WWII Wehrmacht helmets.

Sue Anne and her partners knew that if they were going to succeed they would have to appeal to a different clientele than the meat and potato, heavy-drinking crowd. They decided to introduce a diverse menu to satisfy the palates of both local families and more sophisticated summer residents and tourists.

Then Sue Anne and her partners created a new identity for the restaurant. They feminized the restaurant by naming it Lilly. Next they researched and created a legend around Lilly that would fit into the town records of Rindge for believability. Since then, Lilly's on the Pond has attracted and built a diverse clientele of families, tourists, and business people, and as a result has become a financially stable and growing operation. Local schools have been captivated by the story of Lilly and bring third and fourth graders on field trips every year to hear the legend of the mermaid's return. (See Appendix B for the Legend of Lilly.)

In this example, the story of Lilly was used to alter people's perception of the restaurant. Sue Anne and her partners fashioned a new culture. They understood how important it was to reach people's imaginations. By creating a story tied to the history and community of Rindge, they enabled people to feel a unique connection to their restaurant. The restaurant's success is directly correlated with the staying power of story.

When I think about the role stories can play in modifying culture, I am reminded of the children's album produced in the 1970s called *Free to Be You and Me*. It's a collection of songs, poems, and stories aimed at breaking down the stereotypes of male and female roles. The hysterically funny opening skit says it all. During the skit two newborn babies are talking in a hospital. They are trying to figure out who is a boy and who is a girl. The two babies go through a litany of their likes and dislikes. All the while, the boy, who is played by Mel Brooks, insists that because of each of their likes, dislikes, and goals in life he must be a girl and she must be a boy. Of course, at the end of the skit they are amazed when nurses come to change their diapers and they discover their real gender.

There is another song, about William, who wants a doll. William is good at baseball, and plays with marbles, but he also wants a doll. Or there is the story of Princess Atalantis, whose father wants her to get married and holds a race to decide who will be her husband. She insists that she be allowed to run in the race and that if she wins she will not have to marry any of her suitors. Young John has admired Atalantis from afar and has wanted to meet her. The race ends in a tie between the two. The king declares Young John the winner but Young John replies that Atalantis does not need to marry him and that she should marry someone that she loves and of her own choosing. He asks Atalantis to spend the afternoon with him and she accepts with delight. They have a wonderful time sharing their thoughts and interests with one another, but in the end, she rides off on her horse to see the world, and he sails around the world charting new territories.

Imagine children and parents listening to these stories over and over again. Up until the 1950s, our culture consisted of some fairly rigid ideas about gender roles. Among other things, this album was a vehicle for introducing new values. It's amazing that a few stories could play such a major role in moving our collective consciousness in new directions.

Through stories it becomes possible to see things in a fresh light. Leaders can achieve similar effects in their organizations. They can bring key stories to people's attention and use them to reflect values and beliefs they wish to inculcate in their organization, or they can construct new ones to do the same thing. However, it is important for leaders to ensure that the values and beliefs reflected in the stories they tell correspond to the three other key indicators of the culture: the physical environment, written word, and policies and practices. And keep in mind that it is difficult for an organization to project one image to its customers and have a different set of images, values, or beliefs internally.

CHANGE MANAGEMENT

I was doing consulting for General Motors (GM) Corporation's Information Systems and Services (IS&S) group. This was a new functional area in GM. Given its practice of outsourcing, GM had operated without a functional area dedicated to information technology (IT). As part of the creation of this new group, the senior leadership decided to provide extensive training for all IS&S employees. Part of the training included a presentation by the chief strategist. During the presentation he used the image of a supertanker and a trim tab. To paraphrase him, turning a supertanker cannot possibly be done with a rudder; no rudder is strong enough to withstand the force of water pushing against it. Therefore, a supertanker uses a small trim tab on its rudder. He likened IS&S to the trim tab of a super tanker. This was a powerful and effective way of communicating how he envisioned the work of IS&S. When people begin to question how a small group of IT employees can affect an organization the size of GM, they will return to this image of the trim tab.

Change management is about communicating. If you assume most people do not like change, then change management means helping people envision possibilities. Change is uncomfortable because it is uncertain. We grow accustomed to doing things and seeing things in a particular way. The psychologist James Hillman has a very insightful way of looking at change: He talks about people's attachment to habits. Hillman points out that the word "habitat" and "habituation" have closely related meanings. Habits are the ingrained patterns of behaviors and thoughts that we habituate. Change takes us outside our familiar zone of comfort and knowledge.

There's a paradox here. Change is as natural to us as is habituation. Think about your body. Within seven years almost every cell in your body is replaced. What about the four seasons? There is nothing permanent or stable about life or us. Everything is in a state of flux. The Greek philosopher Heraclitus used the image of a flowing river to depict the changing nature of things. Life adheres to the laws of change. However, our perceptual system is designed to perceive the world as stable and concrete. If it weren't, we would have an awfully hard time walking around without falling all over the place. Accepting this paradox or tension between change and stability is fundamental to our discussion of change management. If you cannot accept that change is as much a part of who and how we are, then it is unlikely you will be effective at managing it.

Change management is not about creating stability in the face of chaos; rather, it is about giving people tools to imagine new possibilities. As a competitive fencer I have learned an interesting lesson about the nature of change. Competition can be a tense and nerve-wracking experience. The outcome of a match is not known in advance. No matter how good you are, or how weak a particular opponent may be, there are no guarantees. Tension is generated by this uncertainty, and for spectators, this is a large part of the excitement surrounding any contest. Since there are two possible outcomes, it is not uncommon for an athlete's performance to be adversely affected when he or she becomes overly focused on either winning or losing. I perform my best when I focus on neither one. I am guided by my goal of wanting to win, but it does not control me.

Stories act as guides in the face of uncertainty. No amount of cajoling or logical reasoning will help people overcome their fears. People have to find their own way. Stories generate a rich medium that stimulates insights and opens people's minds to possibilities. Effectively managing change requires telling stories that move people's locus of attention away from dwelling on the negative and paralyzing emotions of fear and toward the empowering ones of hope.

Powerful stories of change trigger people's minds to envision a path. Once they find that path, it is amazing to watch how they are energized. Consider the following image: walking in the dark in an unknown area. At first we are scared and stumble easily. As our eyes adjust to the darkness and we gain confidence in where we are and how to move forward, what began as a daunting task becomes manageable. In fact, when we reach our desired goal, we usually feel excitement and enjoy a sense of real accomplishment. Using stories to manage change has the same effect.

STORIES AND LEADERSHIP

Stories are the single most important tool for leaders. Tom Peter puts it this way:

> The marketplace is demanding that we burn the policy manuals and knock off the incessant memo writing; there's just no time. It also demands we empower everyone to constantly take initiatives. It turns out stories are a—if not the—leadership answer to both issues. (From the back cover of a book by David M. Armstrong, *Managing by Storying Around: A New Method of Leadership* [New York: Doubleday, 1992])

Leaders do not have the luxury of time. Given the volatile nature of markets and the demands of customers, organizations must move quickly. Leaders cannot afford to involve themselves in the day-to-day bureaucracy of an organization. Leaders should focus their energies on being the creators, collectors, keepers, tellers, and purveyors of stories.

Leaders must communicate a vision and rally people around it. Since leaders cannot always craft a perfect vision, it is important that they be good learners and listeners. This requires gaining people's trust and support. Remember the story of Phil Anderman in Chapter 2? Phil tells a story he learned from his daughter, and then presents a new strategic plan for the company. No matter how good Phil's plan is, he needs his managers to execute it. Phil's managers are more likely to carry out his plan successfully if they connect with him and find him and his plan credible.

I remember attending an awards luncheon at General Motors for IS&S employees who completed a long and difficult training program. President Rick Wagoner gave the keynote presentation. During his presentation Rick told a story about how his children tease him by referring to their household as "e.Wagoner" and remind him that the family should be technologically hip and purchase all of the latest and greatest computer hardware and software. He also revealed how his children continually help him learn more about technology and how much more he and GM need to learn. Rick's stories and participation in the luncheon had a tremendous impact on all those attending. Rick also realized the importance of not just showing up to make a few remarks. He stayed for the full hour-and-a-half luncheon and sat at an unassigned table listening to the thoughts and ideas of IS&S employees.

Although there are many different styles of leadership, the most effective leaders are good communicators, quick learners, and active mentors. Stories are the best way to do all of those things. Leaders like Jack Welch of GE use stories to develop future leaders and to mentor employees. He and other key leaders share their experiences and encourage others to do the same. This kind of openness promotes learning and the rapid exchange of knowledge. Furthermore, it ripples through the entire organization and creates a healthy corporate culture. Whatever positive feeling people may have, or what personal benefits they may reap, the real winner is the organization's bottom line. It's hard to compete with an organization that is always ready to recreate itself by adopting new stories or culling old ones to learn from past mistakes.

PART III

A Practical Guide to Developing the "Story Mind"

Chapter 10

The "Story Mind"

The "story mind" is constantly reflecting. (1) It reflects on personal experiences; (2) it seeks to understand how past experiences shape current perceptions; (3) it assimilates new pieces of information by relating them to existing knowledge; and (4) it synthesizes observations into new stories to understand and explain the world. Stories are the way our minds work. Leveraging their power requires a new way of looking at things. Life viewed through the lens of stories does not come without some discipline. Like a "physical" muscle, the "story" muscle must be exercised and stretched.

This section of the book will help you become aware of your stories. It contains two series of self-paced exercises broken down into personal stories and business observations. Although at first glance it may appear unusual to reflect on personal things in a business book, it is paramount to do so. Our personal stories define who and how we are. They affect the way we think and the way we react to others. We are unaware of the influence these stories have on us. Reflecting on them in a systematic way accomplishes two things.

First, once we are more aware of our stories, we have more power over them. We are not simply swept along by their influence. When we consciously own a story, we can opt for a different one. Reworking a story or replacing it with another does not negate the first one. Rather, it is a creative response to the story and not just an exercise in fantasy or wishful thinking. Reflecting on personal stories and understanding how they shape our thoughts, beliefs, attitudes, and assumptions can lead us to gaining greater control over our effectiveness in organizations. Instead of just reacting to people and situations, we can communicate with confidence, conviction, and sensitivity. By relating and comparing current situations with past ones in our "story mind," we are freer to act differently and decisively.

We strive for objectivity but our rational mind easily loses track of what perceptual filters are feeding it information and what stories are responsible for having contributed to the creation of these filters in the first place. The role and impact of stories in the mind is fundamental to how it works and is pervasive, yet we are grossly ignorant of our stories and all of their effects on us.

Second, reflecting on stories helps us assemble a toolbox. By creating a vast index of stories, we can trigger them more easily. The more stories we readily have at our fingertips, the easier it is for us to learn. We can apply a story from one domain to another. Doing so increases our ability to understand how other people are thinking and feeling. We cannot adequately enter another person's frame of reference unless we can relate it to a similar experience of our own. It is rare for people to have identical experiences. Even when they do, their memories and perceptions of it will vary greatly. There are subtle nuances and feelings that people capture and store. The more stories we have, the more we can tell, and the more we can understand and learn from each other.

A common question people ask me is, How do I create stories? It is true that stories can be created or crafted to communicate a particular message or mood. Public speakers use stories in this way all the time. In Chapter 2 we saw how stories can be used to create an environment, and in Chapter 6 we learned how speakers select stories to bring life to their presentations. However, the real creative process behind stories comes from having a lot of stories and making new connections and associations between our stories and our experiences. As the saying goes, "Never judge a book by its cover." If we take an experience at face value and never probe deeper to learn from it, then we have lost an opportunity to learn new lessons or see things in a new light.

In order to benefit from stories, we need to look below the surface, not just once but continually. Haven't you heard people say that each time they reread a book they discover something new? What has changed from one reading to the next? Do we become more sensitive? Do we bring new experiences to the reading? Have we processed more of the book than from our last reading? My father says no matter how many times he has looked at a score of music, every time he picks it up, he discovers new things. Stories keep us alive and vital. In Chapter 6 we learned that the most effective way to tell a story is to relive it as it is being told. Likewise, continually reflecting on our experiences in a disciplined manner builds and mobilizes a collection of stories.

We are after an alertness of mind. Story thinking engages our imagination. We start seeing the world in technicolor. Our experiences become interconnected with one another. We begin to see relationships among all of our experiences, and we look for relationships among all of our experiences. Our interactions with others take on new dimensions because we notice so much more. We become more aware of what we are feeling and what may be causing us to feel in a particular way. We become more aware of other people. What's their story? Why are they acting in this way? Is there any subtext? Are they consciously manipulating me? How deeply do they believe their story? Where did they get their story?

Whatever we are doing we need to be constantly engaged in crafting stories to generate meaning, purpose, and new theories about what we observe around us. All of this must be done with the utmost humility. We never quite know the full story. Nor is it either desirable or necessary. The creative act is the relentless drive to know. Therefore we should never be too sure or too cocky about our theories. A good scientist realizes that whatever theory he or she puts forth is only a starting point. The real work begins as other scientists test the theory and try to shoot holes in it. As more data are collected and analyzed and new lessons are learned, the theory is revised over and over again. That's what stories are all about. In essence, they are the merger of science and art.

When we use our story minds, we are synthesizing data and facts to render an interpretation. We seek to understand and explain what we observe in terms of what we already know. We mold our observations to fit our knowledge, experiences, attitudes, and ideas. This is why being fully aware of our own stories is so critical. These are the backdrops against which new observations and experiences are assimilated. We have to understand how we construct new stories by understanding our old ones. If we can turn a passive process into an active one, we stand to benefit greatly.

So I am not going to show you how to create a story. I am going to guide you through a process to gain access to your stories. If you take the time to go through this process in a disciplined manner, it will benefit you professionally as well as personally.

There are two parts to the process. The first part of the process is reflecting on personal stories (Chapter 11). I have laid out a number of storyboard topics. There is a brief introduction for each topic followed by a series of questions. These questions are intended to elicit memories. Your memories are the stories that you need to review and reflect on. If a particular question does not trigger a story, skip over it and try another one. Although many of the questions can be answered "yes" or "no," avoid doing so. Use the questions to invite a flood of stories. As you do so, try to recall as many details as possible.

For each topic there is also a table to help you record your stories, along with keywords that will help you remember and trigger your stories in the future, to recall how these stories are connected to others and in what sort of situations they would be applicable. In other words, when would you share this story with someone else?

The second part of the process (Chapter 12) will show you how to use your story mind to observe and analyze different work situations and dynamics. Following a brief explanation of each situation there will be a series of questions to help you focus your observations and get you thinking about their implications. There is also a table to help you record your observations.

The personal topics are as follows:

1. Childhood
2. Parents and siblings
3. Grandparents and relatives
4. Pets and animals
5. High school and teenage years
6. College
7. Teachers and mentors
8. Stories told to me
9. Friends
10. Disappointments and betrayals
11. First love
12. The hardest things
13. Time in the spotlight
14. Death
15. Acts of generosity
16. Hurt and pain
17. Unfair things
18. Moments of joy and pleasure
19. Holidays
20. Food and memorable meals
21. Cars and homes
22. Favorite books and movies

You will want to take your time reflecting on these topics. I suggest doing no more than one or two a day. If you rush through them, you may miss some important stories. It is also a good idea to go through them more than once. Ten to fifteen minutes a day should be enough time. At first you may find it difficult or awkward. By the end you will be amazed at how quickly the time flies and how many stories each of these topics elicits. The next challenge lies in making these stories readily accessible. Remember, you are collecting a toolbox.

Other Suggestions

1. Find a quiet space and time for your reflections. Set aside at least ten to fifteen minutes of uninterrupted time.

2. Read all of the questions before answering any of them. Not all of the questions may be relevant to you.

3. Let your mind roam freely. The questions are meant to stimulate memories. You do not need to answer them in any particular order or at all.

4. Try closing your eyes; it will help you visualize and remember details. Pay careful attention to all of the senses in your memory.

5. Do not be surprised if some memories invoke strong emotions. Do not judge them or try to control them. Allow your feelings to come and go freely and simple observe them with respect.

Please note that any of these reflection and observation exercises can be used in a workshop setting. One or two of them combined with any of the exercises described in Chapter 7 can help people discover and begin to understand the power of stories.

CHAPTER 11

Building an Index of Personal Stories

This chapter guides you through a series of personal reflections. Use these reflections to understand how your past experiences shape your current perceptions, attitudes, beliefs, and behaviors. You may feel that your interactions at work are separate from your personal history but that's not true. How you see the world is colored by experiences buried deep in your mind.

Going through these reflections will help you elicit memories. Your task is to thoughtfully review them, analyze them, gain new insights, and index them for future use. Doing so will greatly improve your relationships at work. You will find that you are less likely to react passively to people and situations. Whatever is happening to you at any given moment at work or elsewhere will be processed by another layer of awareness. This layer of awareness is the "story mind." The "story mind" considers possibilities and seeks to continually attach new shades of meaning and interpretation to the events it observes and reflects on.

During the chapter I will occasionally use a personal example. I think it would be inappropriate for me to ask you to examine your past without sharing a bit of mine. The examples are intended to be brief illustrations. Earlier in the book we examined the important role vulnerability plays in effective storytelling. Being vulnerable allows us to be honest with ourselves and enhances our ability to connect more effectively with others. I am sharing a few of my stories with you to serve as an example and enhance my communication by making a personal connection.

Look beyond the face value of your stories. It's true that some of them will not be very significant. Perhaps they are brief memories. However, many of them will be, and if you examine them carefully, you will likely discover unexpected things. Our personal stories are loaded with layers of potential meaning. If we reflect on our stories, we will discover new lessons and develop new theories about ourselves and the world. Our personal stories help us feel more integrated. Instead of repeating undesirable patterns of thought and behavior, we will be more capable of adopting new ones. Furthermore, we will be able to recognize similar patterns and stories in others. Sharing our stories either through words or actions can help others tackle their own stories to gain new insights.

NOTE ON HOW TO USE FIGURE 11.1

For the sections later in this chapter on personal topics, use Figure 11.1 to capture your stories. There are three columns in the table. Here is a breakdown of the columns and an explanation of how to use them.

1. *Description of story*. Use a few words or short phrases to record a brief recollection of the story.

2. *Trigger*. Write down a word or two that you want to associate with the story. It should help you quickly recall the story whenever you want to. Indexing your stories is a crucial step in tapping into the power of them. Have you ever looked inside someone's file drawer and wondered how he or she can find anything? Large quantities of information need to be indexed and require a good indexing system. As you go through your stories in this chapter, you will find a great deal of information in them, but if you do not have a way of accessing them quickly, they will be of little value to you. An index-

Figure 11.1
Table to Capture Stories (blank)

Description of story	Trigger	Connection – relationship to other stories and possible applications

ing scheme must come from your own mind. Trying to fit your experiences into someone else's index scheme would not work since we do not index things in the same way.

3. *Connection–relationship to other stories and possible applications.* Make a record of how the story relates or is connected to any others. It is very common for one story to trigger another one. Secondly, think about any insights you have gained from the story and about when you might share it with someone else.

Here is an example. I start the process by recalling my personal stories.

1. There is a six-year age difference between my sister and me. The age difference didn't matter since we were very close and she spoiled me rotten. Although we didn't have a lot of money for material things, in terms of attention, love, and care, I was a spoiled brat. Regardless of what my sister was doing, she always tried to include me in her activities. If she and her friends were going roller skating, Franca took me. If Franca's friends wanted to see a movie, she wouldn't go with them unless they agreed to let me tag along.

2. At an early age Franca instilled in me the spirit of entrepreneurship. We formed our company DIACO (also known to its board of directors as "Do It All Company"). There was no task too big or too small for DIACO. If we could make a buck we would do the job. We went around the neighborhood handing out our homemade business cards.

3. Hard work was no stranger to Franca. I remember going to pick her up on Saturday and Sunday evenings after she had worked all day in the Santa Catalina High School office answering the switchboard. She learned how to handle a variety of personalities and dynamics at a young age. Today people marvel at her people skills. Yet few people know all the sacrifices and hard work behind the qualities they admire so much.

4. Through her example, Franca taught me the value of hard work. I followed her lead, and when I went to a boarding high school, I also helped pay for my education by answering the switchboard, cleaning classrooms, and washing dishes on the weekends.

5. When it was time to go to college, Franca was not deterred by finances. She fulfilled her dream and went to

Georgetown University. With a combination of scholarships, student loans, and a lot of work, Franca graduated in three and one-half years.

6. Every step of the way Franca taught me how to dream and how to work hard to bring my dreams to life.

This example contains multiple stories, and it highlights many of the things we have discussed about stories. To begin with, there is not just one story here. There are six stories in our example. As we learned in Chapter 1, stories do not need to be long; even a few words can be a story. Also notice how one story flows into the next one. One story triggers another one, and all of the stories are interconnected.

In the second part of the example we will use the chart (see Figure 11.2).

PERSONAL TOPIC 1: CHILDHOOD
(UP TO TWELVE YEARS OLD)

It's so hard to remember the details of our childhood. The years fly by, and yet many developmental psychologists assert that these are the most important and formative years of our lives. Who we are today is largely the result of early childhood experiences. Our childhood environment brings out many of our genetic predisposi-

Figure 11.2
The Stories about Franca

Description of Story	Trigger	Connection - relationship to other stories and possible applications
1. Growing up with sister Franca.	Sisters	Share stories with young people working hard to achieve their dreams but who may feel for one reason or another discouraged.
2. Being spoiled by her.	Being spoiled	
	Summer job	
3. Forming our company DIACO.	High school	Use stories to emphasize how long I have been working, and how many experiences I have had along the way.
4. Seeing her work hard.	Switchboard	
5. Following in her footsteps during high school.	Dish washing	
	Hard work	Story is related to some of the other following personal story topics: high school, sister, summer jobs, answering the switchboard, dish washing, college, hard work, sacrifices, and dreams.
6. Watching her realize her dream of going to Georgetown.	Dream	
	College	

tions. Many of our habits, thought patterns, perceptions of the world, and expectations of others are formed in these years.

Whether it was wonderful, painful, or just a blur, try to recapture any memory or sensation of your childhood that you can. Regardless of our age, we are all children at heart. Maybe you recall the simple pleasure of playing without any cares or concerns. When an activity becomes an end unto itself, this can cause people to feel a special sort of happiness. Perhaps this is the same happiness we long for and seek in our adult lives.

Questions to Guide You and Elicit Stories

What were your favorite toys?

How was your room decorated?

What games did you enjoy playing?

Did you have any stuffed animals?

Did you have an invisible friend you talked to?

What were your favorite bedtime stories?

What were your favorite foods?

Were there any special events you always looked forward to?

Did you have any birthday parties?

Did you like to pretend to be some character or person?

Do you remember losing your first teeth? Did the tooth fairy come and visit you?

Were you ever seriously sick or injured during your childhood?

What was the most mischievous thing you ever did?

What did you do when you got into the most trouble?

Who was your best friend?

Did you have a lucky charm?

What was your favorite color?

What was your favorite song?

Did you have a nickname?

What was your favorite TV show?

What was your favorite movie?

Did you take music lessons?

What sports did you play?

Were you a member of any clubs?

Were you ever horribly mixed up or confused about any words or concepts?

Did you go away to camp?

Did you go on any family vacations?

PERSONAL TOPIC 2: PARENTS AND SIBLINGS

Parents are truly a mystery. They have such a profound influence on us, but we are very different from them. We are an extension of them, but are not they. We are unique. While we may have similar physical and emotional traits and characteristics, we are not identical to our parents or siblings. The mystery lies in sorting out how we creatively define ourselves. Parents and siblings are like mirrors. We can see reflections and aspects of ourselves in them. As we study them and our relationship with them, we are looking for signs and hints to sort out our self-perceptions of our identity. How have we been affected by our parents? What parts of them are inside us? These are stories that can be rewritten. With our children we try to build upon the strengths of our parents and identify areas in which we want to improve.

Questions to Guide You and Elicit Stories

What stories do you know about your parents' childhood?

What things did you do with your parents?

Do you have any memories of shopping for food or clothing with your parents?

Were you ever jealous of your siblings? Were they ever jealous of you?

What things do you admire most about your parents?

What aspects of your relationship with your parents were difficult?

While you were growing up, were there any major events in your parents' lives?

Did you ever see your parents frightened?

How did your parents relate to one another?

Who were your parents' friends?

What hobbies or interests did your parents have?

What things upset your parents?

Did your parents give you chores?

Did you have an allowance?

How did your parents express affection?

How did your parents express anger?

Were you spoiled in any way?

Did you or any of your siblings receive special treatment?

Were your parents strict?

What sort of rules did you have while growing up?

Were your parents involved in the community?

What did your friends say and think about your parents?

Did your parents ever apologize to you?

In what ways did you try to please your parents?

What were some of the most memorable gifts your parents gave you?

How did your parents express disappointment?

What do you cherish most about your parents?

PERSONAL TOPIC 3: GRANDPARENTS AND OTHER RELATIVES

Although I never knew my grandparents on either side, I feel a remarkable connection to my grandfather on my mother's side. He was hit by a car and killed when my mother was just a little girl, right around Christmas time. My grandmother was left with six children in the heart of the depression. Everyone describes my grandfather as a jovial man. He loved to dance and sing. He also loved to sit around the dining room table telling stories while he carefully cut a single apple or piece of fruit that he shared with the entire family. In fact, recently I inherited the old pocketknife he used to cut the fruit. Needless to say it is a priceless memento. He has been a guardian in my life.

Many cultures recognize the importance of ancestors and have elaborate rituals associated with them. They become a crucial and omnipresent part of our lives. We learn about them through stories and personal items. We have a strange connection to the past. Maybe it's because we know parts of ourselves are locked up in a past we can only imagine and access through stories. Reflect on the role grandparents and relatives have played in your life and the stories you know about them.

Questions to Guide You and Elicit Stories

What was your grandparents' life like?

When and how did your family come to America?

What stories have your parents told you about your grandparents?

What physical or personality characteristics do you share with any of your relatives?

What kind of work did your grandparents do?

What stories have your grandparents told you?

What stories have your other relatives told you?

Were (are) your parents close to their parents? Have they always been close?

Were (are) your parents close to any of their siblings? Have they always been close?

Have there been any family feuds?

How did your grandparents meet?

What mementos or family heirlooms do you have? What are the stories behind them?

If you have cousins, how was their childhood different from yours?

Do you have a special connection to any relative? How did it develop?

Do you dislike any of your relatives? How did that feeling develop?

Did any of your relatives serve in a war?

If they are dead, how did your grandparents die?

Did you see anyone in your family suffer a serious illness?

Are there any forbidden topics or secrets in your family?

Whom do you admire most in your family?

PERSONAL TOPIC 4: PETS AND ANIMALS

I did not have pets growing up. My mother always said she had enough "pets" to take care of with my sister, dad, and me. However, my father is a cat person. Without fail, if there is a cat nearby, it will walk up to my father. Even though we did not have pets, there was always some cat around that adopted my father. The most striking of these was Leo. Leo lived with a whole clan of stray cats under the music building my father supervised on the military base of Fort Ord in Monterey, California. One night all these cats walked into the building. Leo moved out in front of the group and approached my father. He must have decided he liked my father because he turned on the other cats and sent them running out of the building. From that day on, whenever Leo heard the sound of my father's car, he ran out from under the building to greet my father and keep him company while he worked.

Today my father is a proud grandfather. Kirean, his "grandson," is a Maine Coon cat he inherited from me. "Papa," as my parents affectionately call me in reference to my role as cat owner, travels too much and is a deadbeat dad. Now even my mother sits Kirean on her lap and has what she calls "conversations" with him. It's amazing to see how much joy he brings to our family.

Why do pets affect us so deeply? Pets are used therapeutically and have been shown to improve the length and quality of people's lives. I heard on a TV show not long ago a wonderful interview with a little boy. The interviewer asked him why pets do not live as long as people. He said it was because as human beings, we spend our lives learning how to be kind and thoughtful toward others and that animals die sooner because they already know how to love.

People love to tell stories about their pets. Whether you had a pet or not, take a minute to recall experiences you have had with and stories you have heard about animals.

Questions to Guide You and Elicit Stories

What pets did you have while growing up?

How did your pets affect your family's life?

What are your feelings toward pets?

How would you describe your pets' personalities?

Were any of your pets closer to anyone else in your family?

What are some of the funny things your pets did?

What do you recall about the death of any of your pets?

How did you come up with your pets' names?

How did you get your pets?

Were your pets friendly with any neighborhood pets?

How did your pets act toward other people?

Did your pets have any favorite foods?

Where did your pets sleep?

What were your pets' favorite toys?

What were your pets' favorite games?

What animals are you afraid of?

What are your favorite animals?

What animal do you identify with the most?

PERSONAL TOPIC 5: HIGH SCHOOL AND TEENAGE YEARS

Our teenage years can be tumultuous. We go through so many changes in a short time. We are not adults, but we are not children. We are stuck somewhere in between. We desperately want our independence but still require structure, discipline, and most of all, tender care.

What about the transition from middle school to high school? We go from the top of a pecking order to the bottom. How did you assert and define yourself during this period?

During high school we are dealing with new friendships, activities, and decisions. We begin to develop strong ideas, values, and ideals we swear we will always stand by. We hear others say that these are some of the best years of our life, but we have nothing to compare them with. Senior year seems so perfect we never want it to end; or it is troubled, but graduating and moving on to higher education is terrifying. Whatever our experience, our teenage years are larger than life. We awaken to the world in new ways. We hunger to make our mark by finding and asserting our uniqueness in a confusing and often contradictory world.

Questions to Guide You and Elicit Stories

What do you remember about your first days of high school?

Were you a member of any clubs?

Were you on any athletic teams?

What was your daily routine like?

What were your favorite hangouts?

What was lunch like in the cafeteria?

Did you ever get into serious trouble?

Did you have any enemies?

Did you have a clique of friends?

Who were some of the memorable students, teachers, and school personalities?

Who were the most popular people in school?

Whom were you attracted to?

What experiences did you have dating?

Did you go on any class field trips?

What were the most difficult classes?

What classes did you like the most? The least?

What were your experiences with high school dances and parties?

How was your high school prom?

What jobs did you work?

Did you participate in any school shows or concerts?

What were your first experiences with alcohol or drugs?

Were you involved in any community activities?

What was your favorite music? Did you go to any concerts?

What did you wear to school?

What kind of student were you?

How was the college application process?

What mattered the most to you?

How did you spend your summers?

PERSONAL TOPIC 6: COLLEGE

I went to college at Brandeis University. The transition from the West Coast to the East Coast was dramatic. I had never seen the glorious metamorphosis of fall or played in the snow. I had gone to a boarding high school, so I was fairly accustomed to roommates and being on my own, but I was not thrilled to be in school. High school had tired me out, and even with scholarships and financial aid, the only way I could afford to go to school was by working twenty hours a week. I remember reading the list of "work study" jobs. I had washed dishes, cleaned classrooms, and answered telephones to help pay for high school. The thought of working in a cafeteria again repulsed me. In order to get a better-paying and more challenging job, I posed as a graduate student, hoping to be hired as a research assistant for a policy think tank. To impress my prospective employer, I walked into the interview carrying a briefcase. They knew I wasn't a graduate student, but they must have been impressed by my guts and determination, because I got the job.

After all the standardized tests, essays, applications, college tours, and counseling, students are exhausted. It's a wonder we have the reserves to actually go to college. When we finally arrive, we get our first real taste of freedom. Maybe you traveled far away to another part of the country, or maybe your life did not change much at all. Perhaps you could attend college only part time. In my family, going to college was a big deal. My father never graduated from high school and my mother longed to go to college but never did.

In college we are surrounded by diversity. We are challenged to go outside our comfort zone. We meet people with all sorts of experiences and with different ideas and values. We immerse ourselves in ideas and digest huge quantities of information. We develop elaborate social networks, and most important, we add the finishing touches to identities we began creating in high school.

Questions to Guide You and Elicit Stories

How were your first days of college?

Who were your roommates?

How did you decide on your major?

What jobs did you have in college?

What activities were you involved in?

What kind of social life did you have?

Who were your friends?

What were the most difficult classes?

What classes did you like the most? The least?

What was the worst grade you ever got?

How did you cope with the pressure of finals?

How did you spend your vacations?

What kind of study habits did you have?

Did you ever cheat?

What did you do for your twenty-first birthday?

What changes did you undergo in college?

Who had the most influence on you?

What was the craziest thing you did?

What changes did you see in your friends?

What was the best paper you ever wrote?

What did you enjoy about college the most?

PERSONAL TOPIC 7: TEACHERS AND MENTORS

Great teachers leave a lasting impression. They have a way of challenging us and changing the way we see the world and ourselves. Perhaps they know how to push us, or maybe they see gifts, abilities, or potentials within us and refuse to let us sit back and not realize them. Maybe we are moved by their enthusiasm and love for teaching. Exceptional teachers know how to make learning fun. Somehow every lesson becomes a novel experience. They engage our minds and captivate our imaginations.

Mentors are special guides. Sometimes we find them, and sometimes they find us. They share their experiences with us and help us to focus on answering the right questions. Rarely do they give us answers, but they offer us their time, energy, and insights; the rest is up to us. Think about the impact teachers have had on you and the people who have played a major role in guiding you. Then consider how you are a teacher and mentor to others.

Questions to Guide You and Elicit Stories

Who were your favorite teachers?

Who were your least favorite teachers?

How would you describe their style of teaching?

How did they affect you?

How did they affect other students?

Did you ever tell them what impact they had on you?

Were you attracted to any of your teachers?

Did you receive special treatment from any teachers?

What did you learn from those teachers?

What do you know about their lives and experiences?

Did you ever disappoint any of your teachers?

Did any of them disappoint you?

Have you ever thought about being a teacher? If so, what would you want to teach?

What do you think about your children's teachers?

Were there any influential coaches in your life?

In what ways do you emulate your favorite teachers and mentors?

Did they have any favorite sayings or tidbits of wisdom?

How have your impressions of these teachers changed over the years?

Who were your mentors?

How did you meet them?

How did they help you?

How has the role mentors have played in your life changed over the years?

Did you ever receive bad guidance from a mentor?

If you could have anyone as your mentor, who would it be? Why?

How are you a mentor to others?

Have you ever given bad guidance to others?

Do you feel compelled to help certain types of people? Why?

If you could spend a day in anyone's life, whose would it be?

PERSONAL TOPIC 8: STORIES TOLD TO ME

It's magic, and I see it all the time: The moment I say the words "Once upon a time" or "Let me tell you a story," people's eyes light up, and I instantly have their attention. I recall bedtime stories with great pleasure. It was my favorite time of day; I was relaxed and tucked into bed while listening to the soothing sound of my mother's voice reading a story. I also recall running around on the playground working up a sweat during afternoon recesses and coming back to the classroom to lay my head on my desk and listen to my third-grade teacher read us chapters from a book. We protested loudly every time she stopped.

We always love hearing stories, but it's interesting to take note of which ones stick out in our minds. Which ones do we remember and why do we remember them? Stories are hidden containers for our thoughts, hopes, beliefs, and fears. Reflecting on the stories told to us can help open emotional containers we may not realize are even there. Think back on all the different stories told you and what role they play in your psyche today.

Questions to Guide You and Elicit Stories

What stories left the greatest impression on you?

What is the first story told to you that you remember?

What stories did you love to hear over and over again?

What stories captivated you the most?

What stories did you never believe?

What stories did you repeat to others?

What family stories were told to you?

What's the scariest story you ever heard?

What's the most uplifting story you ever heard?

Are there any stories you have tried to forget but been unable to?

What stories did your parents tell about you?

What stories mean the most to you?

What stories angered you?

Did you feel compelled to research any stories told to you? If so, which?

How have you adapted or changed any stories told to you?

What religious stories were told to you?

Which religious stories had the greatest impact on you?

What stories did your teachers tell you?

What stories did your friends tell you?

What is the most recent story that stands out in your mind?

What story or story character best describes you?

PERSONAL TOPIC 9: FRIENDS

We give our hearts to friends and we entrust them with our secrets. They are there in good times, and they are there to help us through our darkest moments. Often they pass in and out of our lives, or we lose touch with them. Sometimes we have a falling out, or what may have started as an instantaneous and strong connection just fizzles. Perhaps we go long periods of time without seeing or speaking to friend, but it has no effect on the strength of the relationship.

We have many associates with whom we interact socially or professionally, but we consider only a few people to be close friends. Friends are so many things. Different friends fill different needs. One friend may be light-hearted and fun, and another may be thoughtful and serious. One we go to in a time of need, and another one we go to in a time of joy.

Friends are reflections of different aspects of our self. Have you ever heard the saying, "Show me your friends, and I will tell you who you are?" Take a moment to think about the roles friends have played in your life.

Questions to Guide You and Elicit Stories

Who were your childhood friends? How did you meet them?

Who were your friends in high school? How did you meet them?

Who were your friends in college? How did you meet them?

What sort of mischief did you get into together?

What were the strengths of these relationships?

How did the relationships change over time?

Did your parents dislike any of your friends? Why?

Who are your friends now? How did you meet?

Who is your closest friend? Why do you consider him or her your closest friend?

What were some of the worst fights you had with friends?

Have you ever lost a friend?

Have you ever had a falling out with a friend?

Have you ever intentionally hurt a friend?

Have you ever unintentionally hurt a friend?

Have you been jealous of any of your friends?

Have your friends been jealous of you?

What interests and activities did (do) you share with your friends?

What are some of the most memorable things friends have done for you?

How have you helped your friends?

Have you ever had bad advice from a friend?

Have you ever given bad advice to a friend?

Are there things you wish you had confided to a friend?

How have your friendships changed you as a person?

PERSONAL TOPIC 10:
DISAPPOINTMENTS AND BETRAYAL

Disappointments can be devastating. When someone makes a promise to us, we expect it to be fulfilled no matter what it takes. Promises are shadows of the elusive certainty we long for in our

What did your friends and family think about your first love?

How did your relationship end?

What was your first sexual experience like?

Has anyone ever broken your heart?

Have you ever broken anyone's heart?

Have you experienced unrequited love?

How did your experiences of first love change your beliefs about love?

Have you ever fallen in love but been unable to act on your feelings?

Who are some of the people you dated?

What did you find most attractive about these people?

Have any of these people remained your friends?

How did you meet your spouse?

What kind of things did you do together while you were dating?

What experiences have helped your marital relationship evolve?

Have you ever been divorced? What things brought about failure of the marriage?

Have you ever been tempted to cheat on your spouse?

PERSONAL TOPIC 12: THE HARDEST THINGS

Life is not easy. Every stage of life has its challenges. Even our first moment of life is difficult. To an unsuspecting infant, leaving the womb and taking his or her first breath of air is a huge undertaking. Sometimes it seems as if problems follow us like dark clouds, never leaving us alone, and never letting us get too comfortable with who and how we are.

No matter how much we may be at ease in one situation, there are always new ones waiting to push us to our limits. An athlete, for example, learns how to respect the limits of his or her body and mind but also never assumes that those limits cannot be pushed. Or take the example of pioneers. They know the benefits of charting new territories. Pioneers realize that the status quo is not always acceptable. They are unwilling to let complacency and stagnation rule the day. Athletes and pioneers may be at the extreme end of the spectrum, but what we can learn from them is that the hardest things are the things that help us grow the most.

Perhaps there was a phase of your life that was difficult. How did you cope with the pressures it generated? Maybe your family moved and uprooted you from all your friends, or maybe your parents got divorced. Perhaps it was a subject in school or a transition you underwent in your life. We do not want to dwell on the hard things, but we want to be aware of how they have challenged us and helped us to stretch in new directions.

Questions to Guide You and Elicit Stories

What things are difficult in your life now?

What are some of the hardest things you have ever had to do?

What are some of the hardest things you have ever had to say to someone?

Have there been hard things that you have avoided in your life?

Are there any hard things you are afraid to attempt?

What hard things have you attempted to do but failed?

How have you coped with the hard things in your life?

What has been the hardest phase of your life?

How have others helped you?

How have others pushed you to tackle hard things?

What is the hardest lesson you have ever learned?

What are the difficult things that you have done that have surprised you?

What have been some of the greatest obstacles in achieving your goals?

PERSONAL TOPIC 13: TIME IN THE SPOTLIGHT

I have always been a ham. I can remember the thrill I felt in kindergarten when I had the only speaking part as the head elf in the Christmas play. I'm afraid my first taste of being in the spotlight whetted my appetite, and it has been downhill from there!

Success is sweet. Whether we are introverted or extroverted, we love to be recognized and appreciated by others. Every person is unique and has special gifts. Sooner or later there comes a time when our gifts and experiences are needed. Contributing them affirms our identity and reminds us that we are special. Perhaps the spotlight shines on us not so much for other people to see us but for us to see ourselves more clearly.

Spotlights are not always large and bright. Sometimes a simple compliment or passing remark leaves us glowing for days. What about those times when you thought you deserved to be in the spotlight and somehow someone else stole the attention and recognition you deserved? Or maybe you were in the spotlight for doing something negative.

Many people have a tendency to downplay their successes or feel that they are insignificant compared to those of others. But we need to keep our trophies polished and out in the open. Knowing our success stories gives us strength and enables us to appreciate and recognize the contributions of others.

Take this time to recall your successes.

Questions to Guide You and Elicit Stories

What awards have you won during your life?

What is one of the greatest compliments you have ever received?

What achievements are you the most proud of?

How did being in the spotlight affect your behavior?

Have you ever been in the spotlight and felt that you didn't deserve it?

Have you ever felt that someone has stolen the spotlight from you?

Are there things you have done for which you have wanted recognition you never received?

Have you ever been featured in a newspaper article? On the radio? Television?

Have you ever purposely given the spotlight to someone else?

Have you ever gone out of your way to try to be popular?

When have you been the center of attention?

Have you been jealous of others who have been in the spotlight?

Have you been in the spotlight for any negative things?

What have been your greatest professional accomplishments?

What do people admire the most about you?

What talents or gifts do you possess that you treasure the most?

What are some of the ways in which you have recognized the talents and contributions of others?

PERSONAL TOPIC 14: DEATH

Nothing fully prepares us for death. Yet we can be sure of one thing: we are going to die, and everyone who is important to us will sooner or later die. It is the nature of things.

When we are young we are convinced that we are invincible. Death is the furthest thing from our minds. Somewhere along the line death shows its face for the first time. I remember my first two experiences with death. I was about eight years old when I found a dead newly born kitten. I was paralyzed and overcome with intense sadness. I thought to myself, How could something so innocent and so fragile die? I buried the kitten and conducted an elaborate ceremony for it, but the image of the lifeless kitten haunted me for a long time. A couple of years later I had my second bout with death when one of my father's sisters died. My mother tried to prepare me for what I would see and feel at the funeral. But nothing could possibly have prepared me for the sight of my father crying uncontrollably.

Life is fragile and impermanent. If everything else is a moving target, at least death punctuates our lives with certainty. The inevitability of death stirs up the desire to leave our mark on the world; we want to be assured that we will be remembered. And that is what stories guarantee us.

Take a moment to reflect on all the ways death has touched your life.

Questions to Guide You and Elicit Stories

What was your first encounter with death?

Have you ever been in a life-threatening situation?

How was death described to you as a child?

Have any of your friends died?

Have you watched any of your friends deal with death?

Did you see your parents deal with death?

When did you realize your parents would die one day?

When was the first time you realized that you would die one day?

Have you spent much time in hospitals?

Have you ever seen someone die?

Have you watched an animal die or suffer?

How have you explained death to your children?

How has aging affected you? Your friends? Your family?

What do you think death is like?

Do you believe there is life after death?

PERSONAL TOPIC 15: ACTS OF GENEROSITY

Regardless of how independent we think we are or want to be, we need the help of others. Our lives are inextricably interconnected. Stare at any object near you and think about all the stories it represents. For example, take your car. Can you picture how your car was designed, and all of the people, technology, and know-how it took to create it? What about the gas in your car's tank? Where did it come from? How did it get processed? We have the things we have, and can do the things we do, as a result of elaborate interdependent relationships. Like it or not, we need each other to survive.

Our first encounter with generosity comes from our parents. Whatever your experience has been, one thing we can say about parents is that we can never repay them for all of the time, energy, and care they have given us. Parents are not perfect, but most of them make sacrifices and shower us with acts of love and generosity.

Throughout our lives we encounter people who help us in unexpected ways. Sometimes help comes in the form of major acts, and sometimes it comes in a less elaborate form in the simple things people say or do for us. I am always touched by the generosity and hospitality people show me when I travel. People are proud of where they live, and they enjoy sharing the uniqueness of their place.

Giving to other people and being generous makes us feel good about ourselves. There is something wonderful, and perhaps altogether human, about helping others. Try to remember now all the different times people have been generous to you and all the ways you have been generous to others.

Questions to Guide You and Elicit Stories

How have people been generous to you?

What's the most generous thing you have ever done?

What's the most generous thing you have seen someone else do?

How have people helped you when you have been traveling?

What generous things did you see your parents do for others?

How have your friends been generous to you?

At work, how have people been generous to you?

At work, how have you been generous to others?

Have there been times when you have failed to be generous?

Have there been times when you have not accepted someone's act of generosity?

Are you actively involved in your community?

What acts of generosity have you performed that are memorable?

PERSONAL TOPIC 16: HURT AND PAIN

We like to forget the painful things. Pain can take many different forms. It can be physical, emotional, or psychological. Pain may not be desirable, but it plays an important role in our lives.

Physical pain insures that we are in touch with the healing needs of our bodies. We have learned from our bodies that if we ignore pain, matters only get worse. In this way, pain is a blessing in disguise. It is a symptomatic indication of something that is more pressing and that requires our care. We must attend to our pains; otherwise they will turn into demons forever haunting us.

We should not bury our pains but instead transform them into new lessons learned. We can be deepened by our experiences with pain. In one fashion or another, everyone suffers pain. It is a common part of the human experience. Others can benefit from our struggles. By being in touch with our painful experiences, we can be more attuned to the pain and suffering of others. There is something incredibly powerful about looking into people's eyes and understanding what they are feeling and going through. Our experiences with pain allow us to reach out to them. However, we must first look within ourselves to examine our own hurts and pains.

Questions to Guide You and Elicit Stories

Have you ever been seriously injured?

What things in your life have caused you pain?

How have other people hurt you?

Was there a time of your life that was painful?

How did you get through these painful times?

Have you ever tried to purposely hurt someone?

Has anyone gone out of his or her way to hurt you?

What painful things have you seen other people go through?

What hurtful things have people said to you?

How have you hurt other people with your words?

In what ways has your failure to say or do something hurt someone?

What pain do you fear most?

What pains have you seen your family endure?

How have you helped others in their times of pain?

Do you have any painful memories that are unresolved in any way?

PERSONAL TOPIC 17: UNFAIR THINGS

"Who said life was fair?" Life is filled with injustices. I'll never forget one of my first experiences with unfairness. I was about eleven years old and had decided to enter the Monterey County Fair children's talent show. I decided to sing *Tie a Yellow Ribbon around the Old Oak Tree.* I worked up a whole routine complete with dancing. There was only one slight problem. At the last minute my father had to work and could not play the piano for me. Determined not to let that dampen my act, I decided to do my routine without

accompaniment. All humility aside, I brought the house down, but the judges decided to give me second place. First place went to a cute brother-and-sister dance team. The local television station obviously felt I had been treated unfairly because they aired most of my routine on the evening news and did not even mention the winning team.

It's a harsh awakening when we realize that many things in life are not fair. We thirst for justice. The younger we are, the more steadfastly we cling to some concrete ideal of justice. Plato was onto something when he defined justice as "the having and doing of what is one's own." For Plato, justice takes on a fluid characteristic. In other words, no set of rules will ever adequately capture all circumstances or exigencies. We come to realize gradually that equality is sometimes achieved through inequality.

Take a moment to reflect on all the unfair things you have experienced. How have you dealt with them? Are there any ways in which you perpetuate injustices you have experienced?

Questions to Guide You and Elicit Stories

Have you ever cheated?

Has anything ever been stolen from you?

Have you been adversely affected by other people's cheating?

Have you ever been wrongfully accused?

As a child were you ever punished for something you didn't do?

Have you ever felt discriminated against?

Have you discriminated against anyone?

What injustices have you witnessed?

When have you benefited from preferential treatment?

In what ways did your parents treat you unfairly?

Are there any ways in which you have been treated unfairly at work?

Were you ever treated unfairly by any of your teachers?

PERSONAL TOPIC 18: MOMENTS OF JOY AND PLEASURE

I hope memories of joy and pleasure come rushing to mind quickly. These are our treasures. In times of pain, hardship, doubt, or fear we can recall all our warm tingling memories to comfort ourselves and be reminded that things can and will get better.

Joys and pleasures come in many different forms and flavors. There are simple joys of relishing a beautiful day or the company of a good friend. Joys also come from accomplishing difficult goals we set for ourselves. If we disengage the distracting and often negative droning of our minds we wake up to discover a world filled with wonders, joys, and pleasures at our beck and call.

Questions to Guide You and Elicit Stories

What things in life give you pleasure?

What have been some memorable and joyful events in your life?

When have you been the happiest?

What was the happiest moment in your life?

What accomplishments have been pleasurable?

In what ways have you shared your joy with others?

What activities do you enjoy?

How have you spent time enjoying nature?

In what ways have music and art brought pleasure to you?

In what ways has your family been a source of joy?

What have been the special times you have enjoyed with your spouse?

How do you seek joy in your life?

PERSONAL TOPIC 19: HOLIDAYS

Holidays are very special times. The daily rhythms of our lives are interrupted by special occasions. We usually share holidays with a community, and even if we spend a holiday by ourselves, we realize that we are connected to others who are also observing the holiday. Holidays can be religious or secular—it doesn't matter. Either way holidays focus our attention in a unique way.

Usually there are traditions associated with holidays. Perhaps these are things we say, do, or eat. These traditions provide us with continuity. We look forward to these traditions because they ground us and give our lives structure.

How have you celebrated holidays and what have they meant for you? As you go through your stories, be sure to include holidays like birthdays and summer vacations.

Questions to Guide You and Elicit Stories

What are your favorite holidays?

What holiday traditions did your family have?

Were there special foods or rituals?

Are there any family heirlooms or objects associated with any of the holidays?

How have these traditions changed over the years?

Do any of the holidays have religious significance for you?

How did you learn religious stories associated with any of the holidays?

What were some of your most memorable holidays?

How have you celebrated national holidays indicative of your cultural background?

Have you ever been alone on a holiday?

How did you celebrate some of your birthdays?

How did you spend you summer holidays?

Did your family go on vacations together?

Have you ever been disappointed on a holiday?

PERSONAL TOPIC 20: FOOD AND MEMORABLE MEALS

Food is a glorious thing. Growing up in an Italian family, where eating was a central part of our daily life, has given me a keen appreciation for food. Eating is a sensuous activity. I am always saddened when I meet people who consider eating to be a chore. You have a finite number of meals in life, and my motto is to make the most of each one.

What role does food play in your life? We all have likes and dislikes. How did you develop some of your current preferences?

I find preparing and sharing meals with family or good friends to be one of the most pleasurable things in life. And when I am not involved in either preparing or consuming a meal, I love to banter with my fellow culinary aficionados about all of the intricate details of preparing one. Meals are one of the ways we celebrate special occasions, yet some of my most memorable meals have not been elaborate at all. I can recall the pleasures of basking in the sun immersed in deep conversation with a good friend while consuming a loaf of bread, a tomato, some cheese, and some chocolate.

What meals have been memorable for you? Think beyond scrumptious food. Memorable meals can be much more than that. They include intimate conversations, dear friends, family, romantic interludes, momentous occasions, or the joys of exploring a new country.

Questions to Guide You and Elicit Stories

What are some of your favorite foods?

When and how were you introduced to these foods?

What did you like to eat as a child?

How did you develop some of your current food preferences?

Are there certain foods you will not eat? If so, why?

Have you ever gotten food poisoning?

Are you allergic to any foods? If so, when and how did you discover this?

Do you have any memories of going food shopping with your parents?

What have been some of the most memorable meals you have prepared?

How did you discover some of your favorite restaurants?

Have you ever gone to great lengths to find a particular food?

Do you recall any particular conversations that took place over a meal?

Did you ever make any important decisions during a meal?

While you were traveling, what have been some of your most memorable meals?

PERSONAL TOPIC 21: CARS AND HOMES

Cars have played a significant role in making the world a smaller and more accessible place. Cars give us a sense of mobility and freedom. As kids we long for that freedom, and cars make it possible. Was it a thrill for you? How about the first car you bought? Think about the roles cars have played in your life and all of your memories associated with them.

Our home should be a sanctuary, a free and peaceful haven that provides comfort and warmth. At some point most of us long to build a secure nest. We endeavor to create a space that expresses who we are. Along the way we may have lived in many homes, and each of them is a rich source of memories. Where we have lived and the conditions in which we have lived shape our attitudes about home today. Maybe it's our first apartment away from home, or maybe it's the first time we lived by ourselves. Perhaps we have vivid memories of neighborhoods we have lived in. Visualize all of the places you have lived, and take a tour of the emotional landscape of home.

Questions to Guide You and Elicit Stories

How was the process of learning how to drive?

Did you like to drive fast?

What are the stories behind any speeding tickets or moving violations you may have gotten?

What was the first car you bought?

What was your favorite car? Why?

When have your cars broken down?

Have you ever run out of gas?

What road trips have you gone on?

Do any memories stick out in your mind of driving in storms or bad weather?

Did you cruise around with your friends?

Did you go to drive-in movies?

Have you ever been in any accidents?

What do you remember about the house(s) you lived in while growing up?

How were these houses decorated?

What are some of your fondest memories about these houses?

Do you have any bad or sad memories associated with these houses?

What do you remember about the neighborhood(s) where you grew up?

Who were some of the more memorable people in your neighborhood?

When did you move out of your family's house?

What places have you lived in over the years?

Have you ever lived on your own?

What has been your favorite place? Why?

What influenced you to decorate your house today the way you have?

What are some of the key possessions in your house today that make it special for you?

Are there any special stories surrounding how you acquired these things?

PERSONAL TOPIC 22: BOOKS AND MOVIES

I can still remember walking into the Monterey Public Library for the first time. I was fascinated by the shelves upon shelves of books that were all around me. Each one was an adventure, and I wanted to devour them all.

Reading is such a joy. Did you ever see a TV episode of the Twilight Zone that featured a banker with horn-rimmed glasses? All he longed to do was sit, unperturbed, in the bank's vault and read. There was a nuclear attack and everyone in the town was killed except for him. The bank vault saved his life. The lonely, distraught banker wanders through the decimated town until he stumbles upon the library. The final image of the episode shows him with a look of total happiness since he is finally able to read in unperturbed peace, except as he reaches for a book his glasses slide down his nose and shatter into a million pieces!

Certain books or movies resonate with us in special ways. Often we can better relate to our own challenges and dilemmas by vicariously working them out through the characters in books or movies.

Or a book or movie may simply whisk us away to far-off places and fantastic adventures.

What books and movies stick out in your mind? How do the characters and situations relate to you? What attracts you to these books or movies? Are there any common themes to these books and movies? If so, what aspects of your life are encoded in these themes?

Questions to Guide You and Elicit Stories

What were some of your favorite books growing up? Why?

What are some of your favorite books now? Why?

What parts of the books did you like the most?

Were there certain books that have meant more to you at certain times?

What was the first movie you ever saw?

Who are some of your favorite characters from books or movies?

If you could enter any book or movie, which would you choose? Why?

If you could be any character(s) from any book or movie, who would you choose to be?

What characters do you identify with the most?

Has anyone ever likened you to or compared you with a character from a book or movie?

If you were to write a book, what would it be about?

If you were to make a movie, what would it be about?

Chapter 12

════════════

Exercises in Business Observations: An Example of the Relationship between Stories and Behavior

In the previous chapter we developed an awareness of our personal stories. Now that we have built a vast and dynamic index of stories and by reflecting on them have gained a richer understanding of ourselves, we can move to the next step of developing our "story mind."

Another facet of using the "story mind" in business involves observing people, work situations, and interpersonal dynamics. As we make all these observations, the "story mind" assimilates the information and develops interpretations to explain what it is seeing. These interpretations are, in essence, stories.

In business interactions it is important to pay attention to all of the stimuli around us. We cannot afford to be centered on ourselves. Good teachers learn that they must be focused on the needs and dispositions of their students. If teachers want to be effective, they cannot afford the luxury of thinking about themselves. Teachers need to be tuned into their students. For example, take scuba-diving instructors. Diving is a safe sport but requires carefully training. When instructors work with new students, they must be extremely sensitive to students' apprehensions and questions. Students are entering a whole new realm of experience and need their instructors to guide them. Instructors must be confident of their skills and focus almost all of their attention on their students. Being effective at work requires a similar focus. Like the scuba-diving instructors, at work we need to learn how to place ourselves in the background and attentively observe everything and everyone around us.

We concoct stories to develop theories about what we observe around us. These "interpretative story theories" guide our actions. Developing a story to explain our observations happens whether we are consciously aware of it or not. Once we are aware of what story we are creating to explain our observations, we can modify it as we gather more information. We do not want to be locked into any particular story because it will bias our thoughts, perceptions, and attitudes. In other words, we act according to what we believe.

If we are aware of what stories we are generating to interpret our observations and of how stories from our past are being used to generate new ones, then we are free to accept these new stories and allow them to guide our behavior. In this way the "story mind" is incredibly flexible and dynamic because it facilitates tactical thinking that lets us act proactively versus reactively in the business environment.

Up until this point we have explored how stories can be part of our managerial and leadership toolbox. We have looked at how stories work and how to use stories to be an effective learner, thinker, and communicator. In this last chapter we will examine an indirect relationship that exists between stories and behavior.

The work we did in the last chapter served multiple purposes:

1. It helped us build a large index of stories to share with other people.
2. It helped us revisit old stories to learn new lessons and insights.
3. It increased our capacity to empathize with other people.

The obvious benefit of the work we did in the last chapter is that we have more stories to tell, but there is another level to the role of personal stories. Awareness of them also gives us freedom to think and behave in new ways.

Carl Jung uses a wonderful example to illustrate the nature of people's behavior. In the story Jung depicts three people preparing to cross a stream. Since the stream is wide, it is not possible to jump across it. Each person approaches the stream in a different manner. One person looks at the stream and impulsively decides to jump across it and take his or her chances on getting wet. The other person decides not to chance it and walks up and down the stream looking for a good place to cross, or even possibly give up on the idea of crossing if he cannot find a good place. And the third person searches for a log to place across the stream so that he can cross it.

Each of us can identify with one of the characters in the story. I know what I would do. My first instinct would be an impulsive one.

I would try to jump across the stream and hope I didn't get wet; if I did, I wouldn't let it bother me too much.

There's a paradox here. On the one hand we have an identity that prescribes many of our thoughts, emotions, perceptions, and behaviors, but on the other hand we are also free to choose how we will act. In the example of the stream, each of us has a preferred behavior. This behavior is somehow tied to our identity. For the moment, let's forget the classical debate of nature versus nurture. Ultimately, I think it's reasonable to assume that we are defined by some combination of these things. Aspects of our identities are encoded in our genetics and our experiences—to what degree and how is not of concern to us right now. Therefore, who and how we are is not completely hard-wired.

We have seen how our experiences are transformed into memories that are encoded in our minds as stories. Although we have a relatively stable identity (evidenced by our consistent words, attitudes, beliefs, and behaviors), we are also capable of changing. If we are aware of our identities and predispositions, we give ourselves the *possibility* of acting differently in situations. We are not locked into one story. Despite my gut impulse to jump across the stream, I am also free to search for a better place to cross it or to find a log.

If I am aware of my guiding stories, I will grant myself the possibility to bypass my default behavior and act in a novel way. As we discussed earlier in the book, if I am aware of my story, I am not bound by it, and I can adopt different ones. This does not mean that every time I come to the stream, I will not jump impulsively across it. What it does mean is that each time I come to the stream, I am free to consider my actions and imagine alternative ones. We are capable of being far more fluid and dynamic in our thoughts and behavior than conventional wisdom dictates. I wish to reemphasize the word "possibility." I am not denying the existence of identity and character traits. I am simply pointing out that there is a relationship between stories, self-awareness, and behavior.

The relationship between stories and behavior is an indirect one but central to our discussion of the role stories play in business. The picture in Figure 12.1 of an iceberg summarizes the various levels on which stories operate that we have covered.

Level of the Iceberg	Description
Telling	We share our stories as a principal way of communicating. When someone tells us a story, we usually respond with a story of our own, and even if we don't, we recall one in our mind in order to understand what that person is saying.

Figure 12.1
The Levels of Stories

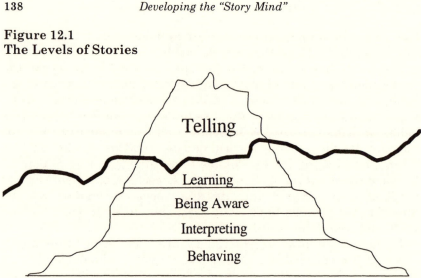

Having many stories to tell makes us a versatile communicator.

Learning

We use stories to transmit learning. If a picture is worth a thousand words, a story is worth a thousand pictures. Complex and intricate thoughts and ideas can be elegantly encoded in stories.

Stories map to one another. We create relationships between stories and look for parallels between them. In this way, stories are also building blocks for learning. We learn by associating new pieces of information with existing ones. When experience remains isolated in a single domain, it is horribly inefficient. As we pointed out in Chapter 1, intelligence is the ability to easily index our vast array of experiences and make connections between old ones and new ones.

Being aware

Since our experiences play a large role in forming who we are, stories are used to gain self-awareness. Our stories contain vital clues to who we are and how we view the world. We need to reflect on our experiences to get the most out of them.

Stories are like watching a videotape of our experiences. They give us access to our memories and provide a medium through which we can analyze the impact of these memories on our perceptions and identities.

Interpreting	We are constantly crafting stories to explain the world. However, it's important to realize that our interpretations are filtered through our perceptions, beliefs, attitudes, and biases.
	The stories we craft are theories. We develop our "story theory" by combining our observations with perceptual filters. Our perceptual filters develop over time as a result of our experiences. And our experiences are accessible to us through memories that are archived as stories in our mind.
Behaving	We use stories to explain other people's behavior and develop strategies for how to interact with them.
	We are also capable of considering alternative behaviors that go against our ingrained ones by being aware of what stories describe our nature and by imagining alternative ones.
	Stories are the templates upon which new behaviors can be projected onto and actualized. We use stories to gain an understanding of who we are. Collectively our stories paint an accurate picture of who we are. If we can access this information, we give ourselves freedom. In other words we can break out of an old story and temporarily adopt a new one.

We don't want to limit the role of stories. It is easy to understand how effective stories are in communication, but this is only the tip of the iceberg. As we work our way below the surface, we discover all the other levels stories work on. This chapter examines the last two levels.

Each layer is built upon the previous one. Learning through stories cannot occur if we do not have a vast index of stories to draw from. We cannot be aware of how our stories affect us if we do not use stories as a vehicle for learning. A key component of learning entails observing the world around us and interpreting what we see. If we are not aware of how we have formed many of our perceptual filters then we will not know how we have come to our current theory. And if we are not conscious of what story we are creating to interpret our observations, we will not be able to choose our actions.

The chart in Figure 12.2 summarizes our discussion of the relationship between stories and behavior.

The rest of this chapter guides you through observing things in your business environment. During the exercises I will suggest things that you should look for in certain situations. You will use all the information gathered from your observations to draw pre-

Figure 12.2
The Relationship between Stories and Behavior

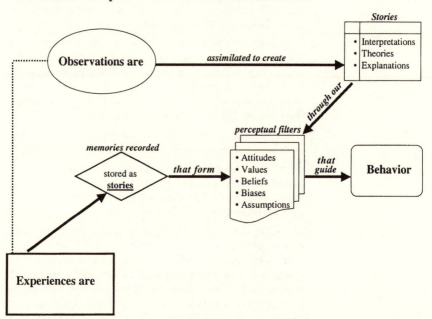

liminary theories and conclusions. Now that you are more aware of some of your perceptual filters, having gone through all the personal reflections from the previous chapter, you can consciously craft stories to explain what you are observing. Use these stories to guide your behavior and plan your actions, as opposed to simply reacting to people and situations.

Here is a list of the topics with regard to business observations that we will go through:

1. First impressions of people
2. Office decorations
3. Telephone calls
4. Meetings
5. Sales presentations
6. Customer interactions
7. Corporate culture
8. The day in review

This is by no means an exhaustive list. It's meant to be a sample. You can add your own observation topics to the list, but this should be a good starting point.

These topics do not need to be done in any particular order, and you can use them in a variety of ways. These observations can be made all the time. Until it becomes second nature I suggest using the following two tables to get started. The first table is used to guide your observations. The second table is used to record your observations and story interpretations. An explanation and example of each table follows.

Here is a breakdown of the two columns in the table and an explanation on how to use them:

1. *Things to Observe.* These are some ideas of things to pay attention to, to get you going.
2. *Questions.* These are some questions intended to direct your attention to specific things. You should try to answer as many of these questions as possible.

Here is an example of the first table:

Things to Observe	Questions

Here is a breakdown of the second table and how to use it:

Actual Observations	Plausible Story	Implications

1. *Actual Observations.* Use this column to record a brief description of what you observe.
2. *Plausible Story.* Use this column to record your interpretation of the observations. In other words, what sort of conclusions can you draw or postulate based upon your observations?
3. *Implications.* Use this column to indicate how the conclusions you have drawn have been affected by other stories, especially personal ones and your perceptual filters. Then decide what story will guide your behavior.

Let's go through an example. The business context for this example will be "first impressions" during an interview of a potential employee. We will limit the example to one group of observations.

Actual Observations	Plausible Story	Implications
Candidate is young and appears eager to impress me.	As an only child from a wealthy family, this person has been fortunate to receive an excellent education. He has never had to work hard and seems proud of that. However he keeps emphasizing how hard he plans to work at the company, which given the circumstances does not seem believable. Although the candidate is very confident and articulate, he is not a good match for the job.	I worked my way through high school and college washing dishes and answering switchboards. Kids who get everything handed to them on a silver platter do not know the value of working hard.
Candidate has very little work experience.		
Candidate describes himself as a fast learner since he never had to study hard to get good grades.		
Candidate made a gloating remark about never having to make money by doing "menial jobs."		I need to find out more about this candidate and ask another person who is not biased in the same ways to interview him before dismissing him as a candidate.
Candidate grew up in an affluent area.		
Candidate keeps emphasizing how hard he plans to work at the company.		
Candidate believes he can rise quickly in the company.		
Candidate has no brothers or sisters.		

In the first column I record some of my observations. Taking note of these observations helps me realize what things are catching my attention. Next I need to interpret my observations. I want to explain what I am observing. I piece together my observations to form a story. The story I generate to explain what I am observing about the candidate was affected by my perceptual filters and personal history. Remember the example from the previous chapter about how hard my sister and I worked and the sacrifices we made for our education? I have a bias against this candidate. I am unlikely to hire the candidate even though he or she may be the right person for the job.

Instead of passively allowing my story to dictate my behavior of not hiring the candidate, I decide that the best course of action will be to let another person hold another interview.

BUSINESS OBSERVATIONS TOPIC 1: FIRST IMPRESSIONS OF PEOPLE

We form impressions of people very quickly, yet first impressions can have a lasting impact on our opinion of a person. Here are some things to be aware of when you are meeting a person for the first time.

Things to Observe	Questions
Clothing	Is it appropriate?
	How would you characterize his clothing?
	Is she well groomed?
Eye contact	Does he make good eye contact?
	Do her eyes dart about?
	Is he nervous?
	Does she seem distracted?
	Is he interested in you?
Handshake	Is it firm? Limp? Rigorous? Warm? Cold?
	Is it short in duration?
	Is it long in duration?
Posture	Does she stand tall?
	Is he stiff?
	Does she slouch?
	Is his chin forward? Up?
	How close is she standing to you?
	Do you notice any injuries or physical impairments?
Conversation	Does he ask questions?
	What does she like talking about?
	How would you characterize his voice?
	Does she gesticulate a lot?
	Does he have speech patterns?
	Does she use any words or phrases a lot?
	What filter words or crutch words does he use?
Facial expressions	Does she laugh a lot?
	Does he smile?
	Does she raise her eyebrows?
	Does his forehead wrinkle when he speaks?

BUSINESS OBSERVATIONS TOPIC 2:
OFFICE DECORATIONS

It's always fun to walk into people's offices and see how they have decorated them. Decorations can quickly tell you a lot about what is important and meaningful to a person.

Things to Observe	Questions
Pictures	Does he have pictures of his spouse or significant other?
	Does she have pictures of her parents?
	Does he have pictures of his children?
	Do she have pictures of herself?
	Are there pictures of special occasions?
	Are there pictures of him on vacation?
	Are there pictures of her involved in hobbies or sports?
Diplomas and awards	What diplomas and awards are displayed in his or her office?
Decorations	Are there any sayings or mottos displayed?
	Does he have plants?
	Does she have any toys?
	What knickknacks are there?
	What posters does he have?
	What type of screensaver does she have?
	Does he put up holiday decorations?
	What type of calendar does she have?
	What kind of music does he listen to?
Organization	Is his or her office neat? Messy?
	How is the furniture arranged?
	Does she appear to be working on many things at the same time?

BUSINESS OBSERVATIONS TOPIC 3:
TELEPHONE CALLS

We spend so much of our time at work on the telephone. We can tell a lot about a person's communication style and temperament by how they speak on the phone.

Things to Observe	Questions
Answering the phone	Is he polite? Rude?
	Is she impatient?
	Does he answer with a formal greeting, or does he pick up the phone and just say hello?
	If she has caller ID, does she greet the caller by name?
	How does his tone of voice change in response to the person at the other end?
	Does she use a speaker phone?
Conversations	Is he doing anything else while on the phone?
	Are she long winded?
	Can you tell if he is listening to the person on the other end of the phone?
	How would you characterize her rapport with the caller?
	Can you tell whether anyone is controlling the conversation?
	Does his facial expression match his tone and voice?
	What is the nature of the call?
	How does she interact with customer service people?
	How does he treat his spouse on the phone? Family? Children? Friends?
Ending a call	Can you tell whether it was a productive call?
	Does she make excuses to get off the phone?
	Does the call end on a personal note?

BUSINESS OBSERVATIONS TOPIC 4:
MEETINGS

It's easy to miss out on a lot of valuable information about people and dynamics during meetings. An organization's political climate and power base change often. Meetings are an excellent time to assess these things and rework our stories.

Things to Observe	Questions
Meeting mechanics	Who is attending, and what are their roles?
	Who is leading the meeting?
	Is there an agenda?
	Are food and beverages provided?
	Where are people sitting?
	Is it an informational meeting? Decision making? Both?
	Did the meeting start on time?
	Did the meeting stay within its designated time period?
	Did anyone leave unexpectedly or take phone calls during the meeting?
Interpersonal dynamics	Did people come prepared to the meeting?
	Who is dominating the meeting?
	Do people appear to be comfortable expressing their views and opinions?
	Are there key issues not being discussed?
	Do there appear to be alliances in the room?
	How would you characterize people's body language?
	What key things were said during the meeting?
	Is anyone acting aloof or indifferent?
	Is anyone distorting information?
Outcomes	Is anyone leaving the meeting upset?
	What aspects of the meeting went well?
	What aspects of the meeting went poorly?
	Was everything on the agenda covered?
	What are the action items?
	Do people follow through on their action items?

BUSINESS OBSERVATIONS TOPIC 5:
SALES PRESENTATIONS

How your company presents itself to customers is key to its success. You need to constantly gauge your customers' perceptions and needs. Observing sales presentations is a great way to do this. The information you gather will help your company continually revise its sales and marketing strategy by adopting new stories.

Things to Observe	Questions
Setting	Who is the audience?
	Where is the presentation being made?
	How many people are attending, and what are their roles?
	What is the customer's expectation of the presentation?
Delivery	Is it a canned presentation?
	Did the presenter assess what the customer already knows about the product?
	How did the presenter involve the customer in the presentation?
	How much does the presenter know about the company?
	Does the presenter use examples and explanations relevant to the customer?
	How much do you learn about the customer during the presentation?
	What sort of rapport does the presenter develop with the customer?
Customer reactions	During the presentation what body language do the participants exhibit?
	What questions do they ask?
	What caught the customers' attention?
	What concerns do they have about the product or service?

BUSINESS OBSERVATIONS TOPIC 6:
CUSTOMER INTERACTIONS

Watching or listening to customer service representatives interact with customers will tell you a great deal about their people skills. In addition you will gain a more accurate assessment of your company's customer service business processes and customers' needs.

Things to Observe	Questions
Customer	What is the customer's issue?
	How does the customer articulate his issue?
	What is her tone of voice?
	What is his body language?
Customer service representative	How does she greet the customer?
	What is his tone of voice?
	What is her body language?
	Is he listening?
	What questions does she ask to understand the customer's needs?
	Do the customers perceive they have been heard and understood?
	Does he understand the customer's need?
	Is she able to defuse a tense situation?
	Does he ever get defensive?
Actions and resolutions	What steps are taken to resolve the customer's issue?
	What does the customer expect?
	Are there any policies or business processes limiting the actions of the customer service representative?
	Does the customer service representative have access to all the information he or she needs?
	Does the customer service representative offer alternatives?
	How could this customer interaction have been handled differently?
	Is the customer satisfied?
	How does the customer service representative feel?

BUSINESS OBSERVATIONS TOPIC 7:
CORPORATE CULTURE

For any organization, corporate culture is very elusive and a difficult thing to define. However, there are things we can observe in the environment that will shed light on it.

Things to Observe	Questions
Office dynamics	Who are some of the people who wield the most power in the organization?
	How did they acquire this power?
	Who eats lunch with whom?
	Are there cliques?
	Do people gossip? About what things?
	With whom are some of the key leaders aligned within the organization?
	Do people trust one another?
	Do people help one another?
	Do people work as a team?
Sacred cows	Are there any people who are untouchable in the organization?
	Are there any business practices that cannot be challenged? Business processes?
	Are there any company policies that would never be changed?
	What are some of the most cherished values of the organization? Beliefs? Ideals?
Legends and myths	Who are the heroes in the organization?
	How did the organization become successful and grow?
	What stories do people like to tell about the organization?
Rallying points	What benefits does the organization offer its employees?
	What in the organization are people proud of?
	How are people motivated?
	How are people recognized and rewarded for their contributions?

BUSINESS OBSERVATIONS TOPIC 8:
THE DAY IN REVIEW

Get into the habit of taking a few moments at the end of every day to mentally run through the day's events. Try to visualize the people you interacted with, the things you said to them, the things they said to you, the actions you took, and the actions you wanted to take but failed to taks. By doing so you will inevitably gain insights.

Things to Observe	Questions
Conversations	Whom did you speak with today?
	What did they want from you?
	What did you want from them?
	Did you get what you needed? If no, why not?
	How did your mood affect your interactions with others?
	Were there any personal matters on your mind?
	Were you insensitive to anyone's feelings?
	Did you say anything you did not want to?
	Did anyone say anything that upset you?
	Did you recognize anyone's contribution?
	What compliments did you receive?
Actions taken	Did you forget to do anything?
	What did you need to accomplish today?
	What did you accomplish?
	Did you hit your targets? If no, why not?
	Did you need to rearrange any of your priorities?
	What's the most notable thing that happened?
	How did you help other people?
	Did you either hinder or get in the way of anyone else's work?
	What effect did you have on others?
	How did other people's actions affect you?
	If you could undo any actions taken, what would they be?

Appendix A

===

Additional Vignettes to Illustrate the Story Paradigm

I have included some additional vignettes as illustrations of the story model presented in Part I. These vignettes can also be handed out and used in a workshop setting as discussion tools.

ADDITIONAL BIND AND BOND VIGNETTES

Vignette Number 1

Mitsu glanced at her watch for the umpteenth time and sighed. It was 6:32 PM. Travel has become such a nuisance, she thought. Mitsu had been trying to get home since 8:00 AM. She had been stuck in her seat for four hours waiting for her plane to be cleared for takeoff from JFK Airport in New York to Logan Airport in Boston.

Two seats away from her, Arlene was finding it increasingly difficult to sit still. All she could think about was Robert's violin recital. In less than an hour and a half, her son would be standing in front of an audience at Thatcher Elementary School giving his first recital, and she was not going to be there to hear it. Arlene struggled with the pangs of guilt she was feeling. She had never imagined that being both a mother and a professional would be so difficult.

Arlene felt pulled in so many different directions. Worst of all, she felt completely powerless. And at the moment, there was nothing she could do but wait.

In a fit of frustration, Mitsu tossed her file of work down on the empty seat that separated her and Arlene. She reached inside her briefcase for a magazine. I should have stayed in New York this evening to see *Madame Butterfly* at the Metropolitan Opera House, she thought to herself. Arlene's eyes caught the glossy cover of Mitsu's *Opera News* magazine. Not normally being one to speak to strangers on airplanes, she suddenly found herself directing a question toward Mitsu.

"Are you an opera aficionado?" asked Arlene.

Mitsu blushed self-consciously, but answered with a warm smile, "I am more like a music junkie." Both women enjoyed a laugh. "Actually, being the daughter of a symphony and opera conductor, I have lived and breathed music my entire life."

"Then you must be a musician," Arlene said.

Mitsu tilted her head back slightly and paused a moment before answering.

"Oddly enough, I am not a musician. Music plays a prominent role in my life, but I practice corporate law to pay the bills. My children laugh at me all the time. They find it ironic that their mother scrutinizes the minute details of contracts looking for legal loopholes by day, and emotes with Puccini and Verdi by night. My kids can always tell what kind of day I've had by the music I play. My oldest son, Brian, who is sixteen and quite a pianist, bought me a pair of headphones for my birthday last year so I don't interrupt him while he's doing his homework."

Arlene broke eye contact with Mitsu and glanced at the floor. "I am going to miss my son's first violin recital this evening. I am a lawyer also, but I am finding it hard to balance my career with my family life." Arlene lifted her eyes from the floor and searched Mitsu's face, which was considerably older than her own, and asked, "How have you managed to be both a mother and a lawyer?"

Mitsu squinted her eyes thoughtfully and began to answer Arlene's question. "Well . . ."

Vignette Number Two

Leonard scowled as he pinned his name badge to his jacket. Why did his boss insist that everyone attend these training sessions? They were always the same, and rarely did Leonard get much out of them. As he found a seat in the back of the room, all he could think about was the pile of paper on his desk. He hoped his gruff disposition would discourage anyone from sitting next to him.

One of the things Leonard dreaded most about these training sessions was the cursory self-introductions. Instructors should realize that everyone already knew everybody they needed to know. Leonard thought introductions were a complete waste of time. Leonard daydreamed about his last scuba-diving vacation in Belize in order to ward off the onset of boredom as the rest of the participants filtered into the room.

With barely a minute to spare, Kevin ran into the room with his cell phone ringing loudly. He could feel icy glares piercing his back. He answered the call and took the last available seat in the room next to Leonard. "Julie, thanks for returning my call. I'm going to have to get back to you. I'm attending a 'Root Cause Analysis' workshop that is starting right now. Do not ask me what a 'Root Cause Analysis' workshop is—I have no clue. I'll let you know when I get to the root of it all." Kevin laughed smugly at his own joke as he flipped his cell phone closed. He looked over at Leonard, who clearly was not amused by Kevin's humor.

The instructor projected the first slide onto the screen and began to address the group. "Good afternoon, everyone. Are your seat belts fastened? We are going to take a trip down Problem Lane. Keep your eyes on the road. We're looking for signs pointing us in the direction of how and why projects fail. Before we come to the meat of the course, I would like to get to know each of you a little better. I'm going to ask you to interview the person next to you. You'll be responsible for presenting this person to the group. Here is what I want you to find out:

1. What is the person's name?
2. What is his or her role in the organization?
3. What projects is he or she currently working on?

4. How does he or she measure the success of a project?

5. What's a fun fact about this person?

"Go ahead and get started."

Kevin extended his hand to Leonard and said, "Hi, my name is Kevin, do you come here often?"

This time Leonard cracked a smile. He shook Kevin's hand and said, "Not if I can help it. My name is Leonard. I'm a product development manager. Currently I'm overseeing the rollout of a new software release, and I know a project is successful when it gets done within a month of the original planned delivery date and when it is 80 percent bug-free. How about you, Kevin? What signs do you look for as you roll down 'Problem Lane'?"

Kevin chuckled and said, "Before I launch into a philosophical discourse on safe driving practices on the road of projects, I think you've forgotten to tell me a fun fact about yourself."

"I don't have time for fun, but I wish I were back in Belize, living on a boat and scuba diving all day," Leonard said.

"When did you do that?" asked Kevin.

"Oh, last month," responded Leonard. "Diving has been a passion of mine for over fifteen years. My wife knows how irritable I get when I'm away from the water for too long. She and the children dread the winter months. They watch me longingly organizing my dive bag. My family has even caught me smelling my neoprene wet suit. Just the smell of it is enough to bring back memories of diving adventures. Those pitiful forays with my dive equipment, along with my grumpiness, prompted them to give me a gift of a scuba-diving vacation in Belize. I'm not sure if it was better for me or for them."

"That's incredible," Kevin said. "I started scuba diving seven years ago when I began working here. I wish I had met you earlier."

Vignette Number Three

Clarence had known for some time that he had to do something about his love life. His work as an independent contractor kept him on the road a lot, so it was next to impossible for him to meet anyone. And because desperate times require desperate measures, Clarence had actually opened a voice mailbox with the Dates for Grab service. He used to laugh at his friends who dabbled in web dating and newspaper ads.

In an effort to screen unwanted responses, at the beginning of his message Clarence read a poem he had written. He thought his strategy was very clever. Dates for Grab charges people three dollars a minute to listen to messages. Anyone willing to listen to his poem for three minutes, and not be frightened off before Clarence divulged pieces of personal information, ought to at least be interesting on a date, Clarence reasoned.

At any moment, Amy would arrive. He wondered whether they would have anything in common. Clarence stuffed his hands deep into his pockets and braced himself for a long, uncomfortable afternoon.

Amy shuffled up to the bench where Clarence was sitting and nervously asked, "Excuse me, are you Clarence?"

Clarence had been so lost in his own thoughts that he had not noticed the attractive woman approaching him. "Ah, yes I am. You must be Amy."

Amy and Clarence exchanged pleasantries and small talk as they made their way to the Museum of Fine Arts. It was Amy's idea to check out an exhibit of Impressionist paintings. Clarence loved art but hated to analyze it. Whenever he looked at a picture, he tried to feel the mood of the scene as if he were standing in the middle of it.

The exhibition was crowded, and people all around Clarence and Amy were engaged in intense intellectual debates. They began to slowly make their way around the hall. Clarence noticed that Amy was very quiet. She seemed to be absorbed. Clarence felt that he should say something intelligent to impress Amy, but when he opened his mouth he found himself saying something totally unexpected.

"Look at this farm painting. The scene is calm and tranquil but I bet there was a storm the night before." Although Amy's face remained expressionless, Clarence continued. "See the little boy sitting on the fence post? He's sad, but it's not because of the storm. He went to his first dance last night and he was too shy to ask Mary Lou to dance with him.

To add insult to injury, he had to stand by as he watched his older brother Marcus dance close with Mary Lou."

Amy's face broke into a slow smile, and she added, "And that boy's mother is going to give him a whipping if he doesn't get the chickens fed before breakfast." Clarence laughed.

Amy batted her eyes flirtatiously and inquired in a teasing but gentle tone, "Have you ever felt like that little boy?"

Amy and Clarence looked into each other's eyes and smiled. This was not going to be a long or uncomfortable afternoon after all.

Questions for Reflection

Before reading any further, take a few moments to think about the following questions:

1. How do the characters in each vignette form a connection with one another? Try to identify the trigger (the specific events, words, and behavior that lead to this connection).
2. What stories do the characters share with one another in each vignette?
3. How do the characters learn to really *see* each other?
4. If the characters in these vignettes had not connected with one another, think of how the events, words, and behavior might have been different.

Analysis

Stories allow people to bind and bond with one another. First let's examine the phrase "bind and bond." Look carefully at this book. How is it held together? What makes the pages adhere to one another and bind to the spine of the book? Is there some glue holding all the pieces together?

Stories provide the same sort of glue between people. In other words, stories show how our sets of experiences, memories, hopes, fears, and desires match with other persons'. I will be able to understand you and communicate effectively with you only when I am able to relate my stories to your stories.

In the first vignette we see two travelers caught in an exasperating situation of flight delays. Each of them is lost in her own world. Mitsu is trying to escape the situation by halting her work and enjoying an opera magazine. Arlene, on the other hand, is fixated on missing her son's first violin recital. When Arlene's eye catches the cover of Mitsu's music magazine, she feels impelled to speak. Mitsu responds to Arlene's question with a "warm smile" and a little humor. The humor eases the tension of the travel situation and breaks the awkward ice that exists between two strangers communicating for the first time. If Mitsu had responded coldly, or more pedantically, the conversation may never have gotten any further.

Mitsu goes on to share a piece of personal information about herself. She reveals that her father was a conductor. By this point Arlene is intrigued. She wants to know more about Mitsu and probes deeper by posing another question. Mitsu recognizes Arlene's interest and sees Arlene's question as an invitation to share more about herself. Mitsu seizes the opportunity and tells Arlene a story.

In a few sentences, Mitsu paints a vivid image of her life as a music aficionado, lawyer, and mother. Arlene listens intently. She sees similarities between Mitsu's life and her own professional and family situations. The two women connect with one another. Confident of the common glue between them, Arlene shares with Mitsu her doubts and fears about being both a mother and lawyer. Hungry for more stories, Arlenes asks Mitsu to share her experiences.

In the second vignette, we encounter Leonard begrudgingly attending a mandatory training session. Leonard's mind is wandering. He is focused on the work on his desk, dreading the moment he must introduce himself to the group, and daydreaming about scuba diving. Kevin storms into the room at the last minute. Clearly, he is also unexcited about attending a workshop on "Root Cause Analysis." During his cell phone conversation, we hear Kevin use humor to make the situation more bearable. Kevin observes that Leonard is more annoyed than amused by his stab at humor.

After a few opening remarks, the instructor asks the participants to interview one another. Kevin immediately extends a handshake to Leonard and makes another glib comment. This time Leonard manages to muster a smile. As he shakes Kevin's hand, he obligingly rattles off quick answers to the introductory questions listed by the instructor. Leonard matches Kevin's sarcastic tone in his answers. Kevin, realizing that he and Leonard are at least on the surface beginning to connect with one another, takes a risk by humorously nudging Leonard to share a "fun fact."

At first it appears that Leonard will ignore Kevin's nudging by claiming he works too hard to have any fun. However, the drive to connect to Kevin, and share his scuba-diving passion, overrides Leonard's defense system. In a short story burst, Leonard relives the personal exigencies that brought about his recent trip to Belize. Kevin is amazed. Kevin and Leonard now have more than a shared annoyance at attending a workshop to bind and bond them.

In our third vignette, Clarence is a victim of relationships in the nineties. Because of his work as an independent contractor, Clarence has difficulty meeting women. Consequently, he establishes a voice mailbox with a telephone dating service. The first instance of storytelling in the vignette occurs before Clarence and Amy have even met one another.

Clarence takes a novel approach to his message. Facts, he believes, are too dry and uninformative, so he decides to read a poem he has written. The poem is an instance of storytelling. Through the poem Clarence reveals a piece of his imagination. He goes on to reason that if someone spends the time and money to listen to his poem, is not made uncomfortable by it, and still wants to meet him, then a date with this person should at least be interesting.

When Amy walks up to him, Clarence is too lost in his own worries to even notice her. At Amy's suggestion, they go to the Museum of Fine Arts. Clarence's mind continues to plague him with worries. Art is an emotional experience for Clarence. He does not like to analyze paintings. Rather, Clarence enjoys immersing himself in the story a painting tells him.

He notices that Amy appears to be very absorbed. Clarence wants to impress Amy. Since he knows nothing about her, Clarence decides to say something intellectually stimulating. But when he opens his mouth to comment on a painting he finds himself drawn into telling a story. Initially, as Clarence starts to tell his story, Amy's face remains expressionless, but as Clarence continues, Amy's face breaks into a slow smile. She responds by adding a piece to Clarence's story. By doing so, Amy is collaborating with Clarence, and collaboration is an important step toward making them partners.

Amy's addition to Clarence's story causes them to laugh. Once again, we see how humor can break the ice between people and ultimately affirm that a connection between them is being made. Amy moves beyond humor by asking Clarence if he has ever felt like the boy in the painting who watched his older brother Marcus dance with Mary Lou. Simultaneously, Amy and Clarence look into each others eyes and smile. Clarence affirms that Amy has not been too intrusive with her question. On the contrary, through the use of stories, they have taken a first step toward forming a real bond.

STORIES REQUIRE ACTIVE LISTENING

Vignette

Gloria hesitated as she picked up the phone to call the Dress for Success customer service department. It was hard to believe she had been their loyal customer for over thirty years. In light of all the complications and poor customer service she had been receiving recently, Gloria found it difficult to stay focused on the positive experiences she had had with the company over the years.

Gloria's billing statements included charges totaling $2005 that were not hers. She had been reassured multiple times that the charges would be removed. However, after five months the charges were still on her statement. Now, Gloria had to call customer service with another issue, and she wasn't looking forward to the conversation. Gloria finished dialing the telephone number and hoped for the best.

Meanwhile, Jill, the newest member of the Dress for Success customer service department, began tackling a pile of unresolved customer issues. She wished she had never taken the job. Jill's mentor had persuaded her to work in customer service to gain a better understanding of the business and its customers. After several months of dealing with whiny, persnickety people all day, Jill found it hard to listen to customers' stories.

When the phone rang in Jill's office, she unenthusiastically picked it up and said, "Good morning. Dress for Success customer service department. This is Jill speaking."

"Good morning, Jill, this is Gloria Vera. I was hoping you could help me."

"I'll see what I can do," Jill tersely interjected. "What seems to be the problem?"

"I purchased a gown four months ago. It's gorgeous, and I have really enjoyed wearing it. Last week I took the gown to be dry cleaned, but when I got it back it was ripped in two places."

Before Gloria could finish her explanation, Jill interrupted. "Listen, Ms. Vera, Dress for Success cannot be responsible for damage done to your gown by a dry cleaner. I suggest you go back to the dry cleaner to resolve your problem."

"Jill, would you please let me finish? I have been using the same dry cleaner for twenty years, and I have never had any problems. On the few occasions when there has been a problem, my dry cleaner has always paid for any damage done to my clothes."

Jill answered in a very agitated tone. "Gloria, we cannot be sure of your dry cleaner's work. Therefore, I'm afraid there is nothing I can do for you. I suggest you go back to them to resolve your problem."

"I have been a good customer for over thirty years," responded Gloria.

"I'm looking at your records and I see an outstanding balance of two thousand and five dollars," barked Jill. "Maybe your gown ripped while you were wearing it."

Gloria had reached the end of her patience. "Are you implying that I'm not being honest? You should do a little research before you start questioning my track record. Those charges are the result of errors and are being removed. If you scroll further down on your computer screen, you will see notes indicating the errors that have been made, as well as the corrective actions to be taken. You will see that I have been waiting five months for those charges to be removed from my statement.

"As far as the gown is concerned, I called to see if we could contact the manufacturer. The rips in the gown are most likely the result of poor material. Since it is clear you have no intention of listening to me or helping me, I will contact the manufacturer myself."

Gloria slammed the phone down and vowed to never again buy anything from Dress for Success. Incredulous, Jill looked at the phone. She wondered if she was ever going to understand customers.

Questions for Reflection

Before reading any further, take a few moments to think about the following questions:

1. Why can't Jill listen to Gloria?
2. Is it likely that Jill's customer service skills will improve?
3. How could she have better handled Gloria's call?

Analysis

Gloria is a victim of Jill's inability to listen. Preconceptions are the enemy of active listening. Even before Gloria calls the customer service department, we realize that Jill does not enjoy her job. Her disposition will immediately make it difficult for her to stand in the shoes of a customer. Jill is not open to encountering new perspectives because she has another story fixed in her mind. Jill's tone is defensive, and she demonstrates that she is incapable of listening to Gloria.

As Gloria tries to explain her situation, Jill keeps jumping to conclusions. In an effort to discount Gloria's story completely, Jill quickly looks up Gloria's account on her computer. However, in her haste Jill does not look at all the information since she already "knows" what the story should be. Sadly, Dress for Success loses a customer, and it appears that Jill hasn't learned anything from her experience. Jill is locked into her story. Until she tries to listen actively, she will keep repeating the same story.

Appendix B

Summary of the Story Model

	Stories are used to	Stories have the following effects:	Vignette or example
Chapter 2	Empower a peaker.	Entertain.	Jack and the story of "Shazam!"
	Create an environment.	Create trust and openness be-tween yourself and others.	Phil Anderman and "The way to eaven is through hell."
	Bind and bond individuals.	Elicit stories from others.	CEO Michael Moore and Mail Clerk Jerry Johnson.
	Engage our minds in active listening.	Listen actively in order to understand context and perspective, identify the root cause of a problem, and uncover resistance and hidden agendas.	King Stephen, Zalea, and the scarf; and Capital Success Training.
Chapter 3	Negotiate differences.	Shift perspectives in order to see each other, experience empathy, and enter new frames of reference.	Overcoming conflicts and the role juries play in a trial.

Chapter 3 (continued)		Hold diverse points of view.	
		Become aware of operating biases and values.	
Chapter 4	Encode information.	Create a working metaphor to illuminate an opinion, rationale, vision, or decision.	Janet Shaker and Sea Point Catering.
	Act as tools for thinking.	Establish connections between different ideas and concepts to support an opinion or decision.	The canary in a coal mine metaphor and trains and telegrams.
	Serve as weapons.		Cold War propaganda and political character attacks.

Appendix C

The Story of Lilly

THE MERMAID'S RETURN:
A TALE OF OLD RINDGE

By Luis Ellicott Yglesias

It was a sparkling spring evening with a champagne moon and peepers peeping.

Ready for a change in our lives and having recently learned that the Old Forge Restaurant, just a couple of miles down the road, was closed and up for sale, the four of us decided to drive over after dinner and have a look.

We had known the place in its palmier days so it was sad to see the parking lot empty, the windows dark, no ducks on the pond and the mill-run chuckling for no one's ears.

Just then we heard a whistling of wings and a loud splash on the pond. Could it be a lone Canada goose, on its way back north?

As quietly as possible we tiptoed out onto the dam where we could get a better view. What a majestic bird, feathers white and brighter than the moon itself! By the mask on its face and the questioning curve of its neck, we knew it had been a swan.

This pleasant surprise turned to consternation when suddenly, a most feminine voice with a melodious but hard to place accent called out,

"Have you seen my Johnny?"

Only then did we perceive her, a diminute woman perched side-saddle on the swan's downy back. The great, wavy mass of hair that framed her perfectly oval face and flowed down to her waist was silvery white, but with rainbows in it, like sea-foam, and what we could see of the rest of her left no doubt. This was a mermaid!

We held our breath and didn't dare answer for fear that any response at all would break the spell and rudely snatch us back to a less bright world.

Twice again she asked the question, each time more plaintively.

Then, at a signal, the great bird shook itself, dashed down the pond scattering tinsel spray, spread its wings and in a twinkling they were airborne, flying due east over Pool Pond, as a light rain began to fall.

For days we kept asking ourselves, could this really have happened? And, if so, just what would a mermaid be doing so far away from the billowing ocean?

Somehow, I felt I ought to know the answer; but, at my age, memory is an unreliable partner, so it wasn't until I woke up one sunny June morning with her name on my lips and a tale running through my head that I was able to solve the puzzle.

Here, then, is Lilly's own true story as told to me more than twenty years ago by a good neighbor and long departed friend, Larry Sollow, whose ramshackle hermitage still stands not far from my place on Bemis Tavern Road. May he rest in peace.

When Johnny Lovejoy brought his foreign bride home to his father's homestead in Rindge, folks wondered how this taciturn dreamer, who as a boy had preferred his fishing pole to the company of other children, could have captured such a rare and exotic beauty.

True enough, he'd grown up tall and straight; but this had been no consolation to his parents, for at no point had he shown any inclination to follow in his father's footsteps, either on the farm or in the woods where the great white pines were harvested to be carted down to the coast and fashioned into masts for His Majesty's Royal Navy.

"Like them, I'm for the sea," he'd always said, and as soon as he was of age, he was hired on a drover on the Portsmouth run and disappeared.

Ten years he'd been gone, with not so much as a word, and now he was back with a lass in tow whose bluer than blue eyes had more than a little of the sea in them.

She was dressed modestly enough and had no baggage, except for a largish and rather smelly sharkskin handbag which she insisted on carrying herself and never let out of her sight.

But there was nothing modest about her hair. Like a blonde waterfall it tumbled from the crown of her head to her shapely ankles and would have enveloped her entirely, except for the simple green ribbon that held it in check at the neck.

Both Lovejoys were delighted to have their wayward son back with a bride he clearly cherished and who was already in a family way. But when Mother suggested ever so gently that Lilly cut her hair to a sensible length and tuck it in a bonnet as local custom demanded, Johnny wouldn't hear of it, grumbling, "Might as well ask her to go naked."

Nor was he particularly cooperative when Father inquired after her place of origin, as it seemed only right to send a cordial message of welcome to the family of the bride.

"They get no mail down where they live," was all he said with a wry smile, for he was remembering, as though it were yesterday, the long luminous descent, hand in hand, to the bottom of the Great Lagoon; how he'd resisted the desperate need to breathe until he'd given in and his famished lungs had received that alien element with a tumultuous welcome of deep relief, for the effect was finer and more invigorating than the purest mountain air.

Mam Watah, Mother of Mermaid Olokun in the ancient language of the sea, had received them graciously enough.

"So, my little daughter, you wish to marry this winsome, brown-eyed biped?"

"Indeed, I do, Obeeneee-mee" (which means "My Queen" wherever her creatures swim).

"And does he understand that he must bury his harpoon upon landfall, give up his whalechasing ways and turn his back to the sea forever?"

Here Johnny interrupted, as politely as he could, for he wasn't used to having a woman of any sort speak for him.

"I solemnly swear that it shall be so, uh, Madam!"

"Be aware, my daughter, that you will be joining your fate to a mere earthbound mortal whose lifespan, I'm sorry to say, is but a handful of years while we elementals were already shepherding waves, romping with dolphins and weaving rainbows in our hair long before land emerged and will still be doing so when it sinks out of sight. May the grace of the Hidden On lighten your path!"

And so the marriage contract was sealed.

Johnny still didn't talk much, but soon made himself indispensable about the place, and as for Lilly, she proved to be an ideal daughter-in-law, sweet-tempered and tractable, but strangely ignorant of even the simplest housekeeping skills.

"Like a high-born lady," Mother Lovejoy reassured herself, but was soon disconcerted to discover that the poor dear owned no other outfit than the one she was wearing!

"What's in your bag, then, dear?" she inquired, raising a quizzical eyebrow.

Caught off guard, Lilly toyed with a strand of her finespun hair for a moment, before murmuring shyly, "Just some things from home, Mother. My national costume you might say."

Then, hastily, "Oh, but it's not the sort of trappings folks'd be wearing in these parts."

"Humph, smells rather like a bale of dried codfish to me!"

This rather unkind comment was rewarded with an appreciative sniff and a beatific smile. But that very same day, the offending object disappeared.

Quick to learn, Lilly was soon sporting a brand-new wardrobe which she had cut and sewn herself, and by the end of that first winter she was well on her way to becoming as capable a housewife at spindle and churn as even the most discriminating husband or critical mother-in-law might desire, though she still hadn't put her hair up.

But Mother Lovejoy quit worrying about what she now considered a harmless quirk as soon as a grandson was born, and her happiness would have been complete except for the fact that the younger Lovejoys seemed to prefer long rambles among the township's many streams and pond to a rousing Sunday sermon, nor were they in any hurry to have young Meerow baptized.

Mind you, they weren't just gallivanting over the hill and dale for the heck of it. What they were looking for was a likely spot to strike out on their own, and they soon found it over to West Rindge, which used to be called Blakeville, by the brook that runs into Pool Pond and out to sea, just about where the Allen Mill was later built. Some say you can still make out the stone foundation of their rugged little cabin shining up from the bottom of the millpond when the water runs clear but I never did.

Well, they had a few years of prosperous happiness left yet, though there was some talk when Selena, their youngest, was born. But Johnny and Lilly paid it no mind. By all accounts, she promised to be as beautiful as her mother, with those same ravishing oceanic eyes and that aureate hair; but the poor little dear's fingers and toes were joined together by a transparent web-like material, more like duck paddles than a proper girlchild's extremeties, a fact folks were to remember much later when hardship hit.

By the time Selena celebrated her tenth birthday, the town had far more serious matters to worry about than a little girl's funny hands and feet!

The year was 1775. On the twenty-third of April, four days after the engagement at Lexington, fifty-four men under Captain Nathan Hale marched out of Rindge Common and headed for Cambridge, John Lovejoy among them, with Boston Harbor and the open sea salting his thoughts.

Did he die, as one report has it, on the seventeenth of July of that same year heroically defending the breastworks hastily constructed between Breed's Hill and the Mystic River in the fiercely contested battle with British for Charlestown?

Lilly never believed it.

"He promised he'd come back, and he never once lied to me," she kept insisting until the very end.

Could've been right, too, for there is a document dated 1777 in which a John Lovejoy requests payment for articles lost at the Battle of Bunker Hill. But by then it was too late.

When news of her husband's death reached town, Lilly refused to dress in mourning, or attend the memorial service, for she expected him back any day; but gradually, the sunny seas drained out of her eyes to be replaced by black arctic ice, and her behavior grew increasingly eccentric, or so people thought.

First, there were the bonfires on the shores of Pearly Pond on the first Saturday of every month, along with the dancing and singing to a drum in some outlandish language that went on into the wee hours of the morning.

Folks had long ago grown used to the fact that neither Lilly nor her children were to be seen in church; but when some busybody hinted that she had actually hired an Indian medicine man to conjure up her dead husband's soul, this outrageous suggestion made sense to more than a few otherwise level-headed citizens.

Personally, I believe the poor thing was trying to keep her spirits up by teaching the kids the language and customs of her home country for which this fatherless family might have to depart right after what was turning out to be the roughest winter on record.

Cold! Folks around these parts were used to cold, and snow, and ice, the isolation and the short days and long nights; but when a quarter of the horses in town died of an unidentifiable disease by Christmas, half the cattle by February, and nearly all the sheep during the next month, talk about Lilly's heathenish ways and Selena's anatomical peculiarity grew ominous in some quarters, though there were enough kind souls around to keep a lid on it, and not a few of them got into the habit of discreetly dropping by the cabin with whatever they could spare from their own diminishing larders such as a hardly withered pumpkin, or a pannikin of freshly baked Johnnycake and the inevitable jug of sparkling cider, kindly given and gratefully received.

Now, the whole thing would have likely blown over except for the fact that March brought no redeeming rains in its windy train, and April was as withered as the last apple in the apple barrel. May was no kinder, and what with the British threat, Indian raids, and Lilly's peculiar behavior, patience was wearing thin and some went so far as to claim that this latest calamity was proof positive that the stranger in their midst was a menace to one and all.

Then scandal broke: Lilly and her brood were spotted swimming and lurking about like frisky otters in Pool Pond's crystal waters without a stitch on. It's hard to know which was more shocking, such levity during trying times, the utterly unheard of nudity, or the natatorial skills of all concerned in an era when few, especially women, could swim and more than one pond bore the name of some unfortunate who, slipping on a log, had drowned therein.

That was when the parson, who had fiercely defended Lilly's inalienable right to worship and mourn according to her conscience, but fearing imminent tragedy, prevailed upon the elder Mrs. Lovejoy to pay her daughter-in-law a visit for the purpose of urging she mend her upsetting ways; otherwise she and her little ones might be warned out of town as undesirables.

When Johnny's mother came jouncing down the footpath in a cloud of dust, Lilly was sitting by the cabin door sewing some sort of garment which was narrower than a skirt and shorter than a blouse and sparkled in the harsh sunlight like a hooked shiner breaking water; but exactly what it was she had no opportunity to ascertain because, as soon as she saw her, the startled seamstress quickly stuffed it into the all-but-forgotten and more-fragrant-than-ever sharkskin bag which lay at her feet.

Patiently and with her usual good manners, Lilly listened to her mother-in-law's remonstrations, though she could scarce repress a smile every time the old lady's nose gave an involuntary twitch, rather like a slumbering dog troubled by a pesky fly.

Mrs. Lovejoy's rather lengthy speech was followed by a brief silence during which Lilly scooped up a handful of dust and thoughtfully let it trickle through her fingers. Then, pointing to the result, she replied.

"Yon parched pile, Mother dear, might just as well be my heart! While Johnny was by us, it was full and moist and warm, and I truly believed we could become one of you who have been so patient with us who are of a different order and for the sea. But now that he's been gone so long, even your generous land is grieving with us, and I cannot permit that. Please inform parson that I shall trouble the town no longer."

Round about midnight, when the long-prayed-for rain began to fall gentle and steady, everyone went crazy. Soon people were rushing out of their houses, stomping on puddles and rolling in sweet mud, shouting halleluyas. But no one, not even Mrs. Lovejoy, gave Lilly a thought.

Next afternoon, when the sun came out from behind the clouds, looking for all the world like it was wearing a spanking new Sunday-go-to-meeting outfit, and Johnny's mother jubilantly rushed down to the little cabin by Pool Pond full of good cheer, confident that at least she could persuade Lilly to move back to the comparative safety of her own house, there was not a soul to be found, but the sharkskin bag was lying empty and open on the ground, only now it was as tangy and sweet smelling as a newborn wave on its way to the shore.

Lilly was gone, taking her brood with her, though not for good, because she does drop in on us from time to time, with the first freshets of Spring, still looking for her Johnny.

We dedicate our new restaurant to her and invite you to share Lilly's bounty with us.

NOTE

This story is reproduced by permission of the author, Luis Ellicott Yglesias.

Appendix D

Ordering Story Cards and Obtaining More Information

For more information about story consulting or to order a set of fifty-two story cards contact:

Terrence Gargiulo
781-894-4381
info@makingstories.net

Suggested Reading

Abrahams, Roger D. *African Folktales*. New York: Pantheon Books, 1983.

Armstrong, David M. *Managing by Storying Around: A New Method of Leadership*. New York: Doubleday, 1992.

Benton, D. A. *Lions Don't Need to Roar*. New York: Warner Books, 1992.

Bushnaq, Inea. *Arab Folktales*. New York: Pantheon Books, 1986.

Caldecott, Moyra. *Myths of the Sacred Tree*. Rochester, Vt.: Destiny Books, 1993.

Calvino, Italo. *Italian Folktales*. Translated by George Martin. New York: Harcourt Brace Jovanovich, 1980.

Campbell, Joseph. *The Power of Myth with Bill Moyers*. New York: Doubleday, 1988.

Canfield, Jack, and Jacqueline Miller. *Heart at Work: Stories and Strategies for Building Self-Esteem and Reawakening the Soul at Work*. New York: McGraw-Hill, 1996.

Chinen, Allan B. *In the Ever After: Fairy Tales and the Second Half of Life*. Wilmette, Ill.: Chiron Publications, 1989.

———. *Once upon a Midlife: Classic Stories and Mythic Tales to Illuminate the Middle Years*. New York: Tarcher/Putnam, 1992.

Creighton, Helen. *A Folk Tale Journey*. Wreck Cove, Cape Breton Island, Nova Scotia, Canada: Breton Books, 1993.

Denning, Stephen. *The Springboard: How Storytelling Ignites Action in Knowledge-Era Organizations*. Boston: Butterworth-Heinemann, 2001.

Dorson, Richard M. *Folk Legends of Japan*. Rutland, Vt.: Charles E. Tuttle Company, 1962.

Erdoes, Richard, and Alfonso Ortiz. *American Indian Myths and Legends*. New York: Pantheon Books, 1984.

Feinstein, David, and Stanley Krippner. *The Mythic Path.* New York: Tarcher/Putnam, 1997.

Gardner, Howard. *Leading Minds: An Anatomy of Leadership.* New York: Basic Books, 1996.

Jensen, Bill. *Simplicity: The New Competitive Advantage in a World of More, Better, Faster.* Cambridge, Mass.: Perseus Books, 2000.

La Fontaine, Jean de. *A Hundred Fables of La Fontaine.* New York: Greenwich House, 1983.

Livo, Norma. *Troubadours's Storybag: Musical Folktales of the World.* Golden, Colo.: Fulcrum, 1996.

Macy, Joanna. *World As Lover, World As Self.* Berkeley, Calif.: Parallax Press, 1991.

Maguire, Jack. *The Power of Personal Storytelling: Spinning Tales to Connect with Others.* New York: Tarcher/Putnam, 1998.

Meade, Erica Helm. *Tell It by Heart: Women and the Healing Power of Story.* Chicago: Open Court, 1995.

Morgan, Gareth. *Imaginization: New Mindsets for Seeing, Organizing, and Managing.* Thousand Oaks, Calif.: Sage, 1993.

———. *Images of Organizations: The Executive Edition.* San Francisco: Berett-Koehler Publishers; Sage, 1998.

Parkin, Margaret. *Tales for Trainers: Using Stories and Metaphors to Facilitate Learning.* London: Kogan Page, 1998.

Phelps, Ethel Johnston. *The Maid of the North: Feminist Folk Tales from Around the World.* New York: Henry Holt and Company, 1981.

Pourrat, Henri. *French Folktales.* New York: Pantheon Books, 1989.

Sawyer, Ruth. *The Way of the Sotryteller.* New York: Penguin Books, 1976.

Schank, Roger. *Tell Me a Story: A New Look at Real and Artificial Memory.* Evanston, Ill.: Northwestern University Press, 1995.

———. *Virtual Learning: A Revolutionary Approach to Building a Highly Skilled Workforce.* New York: McGraw-Hill, 1997.

Simons, Annette. *The Story Factor.* Cambridge, Mass.: Perseus Publishing, 2001.

Stone, Richard. *The Healing Art of Storytelling: A Sacred Journey of Personal Discovery.* New York: Hyperion, 1996.

Tichy, Noel M., with Eli Cohen. *The Leadership Engine: How Winning Companies Build Leaders at Every Level.* New York: HarperCollins, 1997.

Wolkstein, Diane. *The Magic Orange Tree and Other Haitian Folktales.* New York: Schocken Books, 1978.

Zeitlin, Steve. *Because God Loves Stories: An Anthology of Jewish Storytelling.* New York: Touchstone, 1997.

Index

Ability to understand, 17
Abstractions, 62, 70
Access your stories, how to, 101–103
Acquiring new skills, 48
Actions, 68
Active listening, 7, 19–29, 30, 33,
    42, 50, 56, 64, 158–161,163;
    preconceptions enemy of, 160
Actual observations, 141–142
Adapting stories, 3, 24
Agendas: hidden 30, 163; pushing
    your own, 65; someone else's,
    36
Analogies, thinking of, 34
Analyzing a story, 62, 81–83
Appraisals: performance, 48–49;
    process and tools, 49
Artificial intelligence, 6
Assumptions, 140
Attitudes, 105, 139, 140
Audience, engaging the, 12, 18, 59

Behaving, in levels of stories, 139
Behavior: 105, 142; default, 137;
    relationship between stories
    and, 135–150
Beliefs, 88, 92, 105, 139, 140

Benefiting from stories, 100–101
Biases, 139, 140; operating, 30,
    163
Binding and bonding: individuals,
    7, 16–18, 156–158, 163;
    process, 46
Body language, 57, 59
Building rapport, 48, 61
Business: defining, 81; interac-
    tions, 135; processes, 8, 88;
    role of stories in, 79–86
Business observations, 99, 135–150
Business opportunity, 84

Candidate employee, 42–46, 142
Change, 3, 8; corporate, 79;
Change management, 41, 87, 88,
    92–94; capable of, 137; is
    about communicating, 92;
    helping employees manage, 87
Clichés, 69–70
Coaching, informal: employee
    orientation, 48
Collecting stories, 81–83
Communicate, desire to, 55–56, more
    effectively, 87, 156; a particular
    mood or message, 100

Communicating, stories as a personal way, 137

Communication, 6, 7, 42, 105; breakdown, 49–50; didactic forms, 61; stories fundamental, 3; stories part of, 62; stories the principal way of, 137; through stories, 90; tools, 8

Communications: department, 43; verbal, 25; written, 25

Competency, 80; modeling, 41

Conflict: process, 29; resolution, 49–51

Connect, desire to, 55–56

Connecting, 4

Connection-relationship, 106–107

Constructing: an image, 43; a story, 43

Corporate culture, 41, 79, 87, 88–92; build or modify, 87, 90; change, 79; comprises values and beliefs, 88; healthy, 95; leadership, 79; modification, 90

Creating relationships, 138

Creative acts, 100–101

Creative solutions, generating, 37

Culture, corporate. *See* Corporate culture

Curriculum developers, 8

Data: structured, 85; understand, 85

Decision-making process, 29

Defining: the, characteristic of the "story mind," 15; a story, 46

Description of a story, 106

Dialogue: pattern of, 54; story, 71–72

Dialoguing, mechanism for, 49

Didactic training, 54

Differences, negotiating, 7, 29–30, 163

Discipline of synthesizing information, 29

Discuss a story, 59–60

Dissemination and sharing of knowledge, 88

Distinctive imagery, 34

Elicit: from a group, 56–57; from others, 18, 163; how to, stories, 81–83; stories from employees, 49;

Emotions, 57

Empathy, 30, 62, 163

Employee orientation: coaching-informal time, 48; informational time, 47; structural-formal, 46–47; unstructured time, 47–48

Employee: experiences, 47–48; orientation, 46–48; performance, 48–49; prospective, 42–46; relations, 17; types of actions, 46–48

Employees: helping, manage change, 87; inspiring, 18

Empowering a speaker, 7, 11–12, 163

Encoding: stories in the mind, 137; thoughts, 138

Encoding information, 7, 37, 62

Engaging our minds, 7, 19–29, 30, 163

Engaging the audience, 12, 18, 59

Environment: characterizing, 88; creating, 7; physical, 88, 92

Exaggerations, 35

Experiences, 35, 37 100–101, 137, 138, 140, 156; employee, 47–48; learning results from piecing together, 35; personal, 99; transformed into memories, 137

Explaining perspective, 29

Facilitation, stories central to, 60

Facilitator, 55, 60; story, 50

Feelings, manipulating, 35–36

Generating creative solutions, 37

Groupware, 47, 84

Healing: process, 36; stories bring about, 7, 36–37

Hidden agendas, 30

Human resource managers, 8
Human resources, 88; the role stories play in, 41–51

Images: constructing, 43, 92; eliciting, 4
Imagination, 7, 34; stimulating, 15
Imaging, 4
Impact of stories, 35–36
Implications, 141–142
Index of personal stories, 105–133, 135, 136
Inducing reflection, 18
Information: encoding, 7, 33, 62, 164; indexing, 4; synthesizing, 15
Institutional memory, 81
Intelligence, 6, 7, 69; artificial, 6
Intentions, 6
Interactions, business, 135
Internet, 41
Interpretation, 101
Interpretative story theory, 136
Interpreting, in levels of stories, 139
Interviewing, 43–46

Jung, Carl, 136
Justifying perspective, 29

Knowledge, 6, 47; managing the dissemination and sharing of, 88; Leadership promotes learning and exchange of, 95
Knowledge management, 41, 47, 79–86; defining, 84; relationship between stories and, 79; role of stories in, 79–86; sharing, 48; software packages, 47

Leaders, 34
Leadership, 87, 88, 94–95; corporate, 79, promotes learning and exchange of knowledge, 95
Learning, 5, 7, 35, 95; in levels of stories, 138; observations as component of, 139; stories fundamental to, 3, stories transmit, 138

Levels of stories, 137–139; behaving, 139; being aware, 138; interpreting, 139; learning, 138; telling, 137
Lies, 35–36
Listening, active, 7, 19–29, 30, 33, 42, 50, 56, 64, 158–161, 163; preconceptions enemy of, 160

Management: change, 41; knowledge, 41, 47
Managers, 18, 46, 84; human resource, 8, training, 8
Managing the dissemination and sharing of knowledge, 88
Manipulating thought and feelings, 35–36
Manipulative stories, 36
Meaning, 33
Mechanism for dialoguing, 49
Memories, 62, 71, 105, 138, 156; experiences transformed into, 137
Memory, 7
Metaphor: creating, 37; thinking of, 37
Modeling, competency, 41
Motivational taskers, 18
Motivations, 36

Negotiating differences, 7, 29–30, 163
Nondefinition of stories, 5
Nonlinear approach, 47

Observations: actual, 141–142; business, 99, 135–150
Operating biases and values, 30
Opportunity for reflection, 14
Orientation, employee, 46–48

Pattern of participation, 54
Perceptions, 62, 71, 89, 91, 105, 139
Performance: change, 57; appraisals, 48–49; employee, 48–49; process and tools, 49; quantifying, 48–49

Personality, 55
Personal reflections, a guide
    through, 105–133
Personal stories, 105–133
Perspectives: embracing other, 37;
    explaining and justifying, 29;
    employee, 46; other people's,
    30, 49–50; shift in, 163;
    understanding, 30, 163
Plato, 35
Plausible story, 141
Points of view: diverse, 30, 37,
    164; others', 30, 49–50
Policies, 89, 92
Practices, 89, 92
Premise of stories, 6
Presenting, 4
Process improvement, 83
Prompts, story, 68
Propaganda, 35–36
Pubic relations, 43

Quantifying employee perfor-
    mance, 48–49

Rapport building, 48, 61
Rational mind as opposed to the
    story mind, 24
Recruiters, 42
Recruiting, 41–43, 83; strategies,
    43
Reflecting on personal stories,
    101–102
Reflection: inducing, 18; opportu-
    nity for, 12
Reflections: a guide through
    personal, 105–133
Reflective process, 55
Relations, employee, 17
Relationship: between stories and
    behavior, 135–150; between
    stories and knowledge, 79
Relationships, 8, 62, 75, 101;
    creating 138
Repetition, 58
Restructuring, 84
Resume, 43
Role: in conflict resolutions, 49–51;

in employee orientation,
    46–48; in interviewing, 43–46;
    in performance appraisals,
    48–49; in recruiting, 41–43;
    stories can play in business,
    137–139; of stories in business
    processes, 79–86; stories can
    play, 41–51; of stories in
    knowledge management,
    79–86; vulnerability, 61, not
    wanting to limit the, of
    stories, 139
Roles, 68

Schank, Roger, 5, 69
Sensitivity, 55–57; to moods,
    needs and desires, 55–57
Sharing and dissemination of
    knowledge, 88
Simplification, 83
Skills, acquiring new, 48
Solutions, generating creative, 37
Speaker(s): empowering, 7, 11–12,
    163; memorable, 12
Staff development, 5
Stories:
    accessing your, 101–103
    adapt, 24
    analyzing, 62
    benefiting from, 100–101
    best gauge of organizations
        culture, 89
    bind and bond individuals, 7,
        16–18, 156, 158–163
    bring about healing, 7, 36–37
    building an index of personal,
        105–133
    business observations and, 99
    in business, 4
    central to training and facilita-
        tion, 60
    communicating, a personal way
        of, 137
    constructing, 43
    create an environment, 7, 12–16,
        55–56, 163
    create trust, 163
    defining, 46, 90

description, 6
develop the discipline of synthe-
　sizing information, 15
discussion, 59–60, 88
effective, 43
effective thinking tools, 34–35
effects of, 7
elicit images, 4
eliciting, 81–83
eliciting from employees, 42, 49
eliciting from others, 18, 163
empower a speaker, 7, 11–12,
　163
encode information, 7, 31–34,
　62, 164
engage our minds in active
　listening, 7, 19–29, 163
entertain, 18, 163
equip our minds with templates
　for thinking, 34
evolve, 24
facilitator of, 50
fundamental to communication, 3
fundamental to learning, 3
as guides, 93
help assemble a toolbox, 99–100
how to tell, 54–59, 88, 101
improve communication, 53
index information, 4
index of personal, 105–133, 135
integrate people into a group, 53
leadership and, 94–95
levels of operation, 137–139
limiting, not wanting to limit
　the role of, 139
listening to, 61
manipulative, 36
mechanism for dialoguing, 49
multiple and conflicting points
　of view, 29
negotiate differences, 7, 29–30,
　163
nondefinition of, 5
not linear in nature, 29
observations, business, and, 99
participation in, 59
personal, 99, 105–133
plausible, 140–141

power of, 4, 5
practice telling, 61–77
premise of, 6
as propaganda, 35
reflecting on personal, 101–102
relate mine to yours, 17
relationship to knowledge, 79
relevance of, 14
reliving, 58–59
repetition in, 58, 62
role of, in business processes,
　79–86
role in business, 137–139
role conflict resolution, 49–51
role in corporate culture, 87,
　88–92
role in employee orientation,
　46–48
role in interviewing, 43–46
role in knowledge management,
　79–86
role in performance appraisals,
　48–49
role in recruiting, 41–43
roles, play, 41–51, 79–86,
　137–139
selection, 54–55, 88
telling, 61–77, 137
templates for projecting and
　actualizing our behaviors, 139
templates for thinking, 34
thinking, 62
tools for thinking, 7, 34–35, 164
in training, 53–60
triggering, 62, 68, 70, 93, 100
use determines impact, 35–36
using, to modify a culture, 90
as weapons, 7, 35–36, 164
Story cards, 72–75, 173
Story dialogue, 71–72
Story listening, 88
Story mind, 99–103. 105, 135–136;
　defining characteristic, 15; use
　in observation and analysis,
　102–103
Story model, 8, 30, 37
Story prompts, 68
Story skills, 88; developing, 61–77

Storytelling, 36, 61–62, 86
Story thinking, 35, 87, 88, 101
Story workshops, 61
Strategies, recruiting, 43
Structured data, 85

Tactical thinking, 136
Team building, 5
Telling a story: how to, 54–59; practice, 61–77
Telling, in levels of stories, 137
Templates, 139; for projecting and actualizing our behaviors, 139; for thinking, 34
Thinking analogically, 35; in stories, 62; of an analogy or metaphor, 34; tactical, 136; templates for 34
Thoughts, 6; manipulating 35–36
Tone of communication, 28
Toolbox, stories help assemble, 99–100
Tools for thinking, 7, 37, 164
Training, 41, 83; didactic, 54, informational, 54; managers, 8, 28; stories central to, 60; stories in, 53–60; workshops, 18

Trigger, 106
Trust, 48; creating, 163
Truth of a story, 8
Twain, Mark, 10

Understanding: business processes, 79–86; context, 30; knowledge management, 79–86; a new realm, 24; perspective, 30; relationships between memories, perceptions, and stories, 62
Unstructured data, 85
Unstructured time, employee orientation, 47–48

Values, 6, 88, 92, 140; operating, 30, 163
Verbal: communication, 25; instructions, 48
Voice, 58

Weapons, stories as, 7, 35–36, 164
Word story, 35
Written: communication, 25; word, 92

Yglesias, Luis, 165

ABOUT THE AUTHOR

Terrence L. Gargiulo is a management consultant, organizational development specialist, and group process facilitator based in San Francisco, CA. He holds a Master of Management in Human Services from the Florence Heller School, Brandeis University, and is a recipient of Inc. Magazine's Marketing Master Award. Among his numerous clients, past and present, are General Motors, Merck, Arthur D. Little, Raytheon, Coca-Cola, and the National Association of Manufacturers.